THE YOUNG PEACE MAKER

THE YOUNG PEACE MAKER

CORLETTE SANDE

HEY, COACH, WHY DON'T YOU INVITE THE UMP TO YOUR **PEACEMAKING** CLASS?

illustrated & designed
by **Russ Flint & Associates**

Permission to Reproduce

If you purchase this manual, you are granted permission to photocopy the appendices for each of the students in your home or classroom. If you purchase both this manual and a set of Student Activity Books, you are also granted permission to photocopy the Student Activity Books for each of the students in your home or classroom.

©1997 by Corlette Sande

Developed by Peacemaker Ministries®
1537 Avenue D, Suite 325
Billings, MT 59102
Phone: (406) 256.1583
E-mail: mail@hispeace.org
Web site: www.hispeace.org

The Young Peacemaker is published by Shepherd Press
PO Box 24
Wapwallopen, PA 18660
Phone: (800) 338-1445
E-mail: info@shepherdpress.com
Web site: www.shepherdpress.com

Unless indicated otherwise, all Scripture quotations are taken from the Holy Bible, New International Version ®. Copyright © 1973, 1978, 1984 by International Bible Society. Used by permission of Zondervan Publishing House. All rights reserved.

ISBN 0-9663786-1-X (previously 0-9659889-0-2)

Printed in the United States of America

Table of Contents

Blessed

are the peace- makers, for they will be called sons of God.

Matthew 5:9

I had only been on the telephone for two minutes when the screaming started in my living room. Megan, my four-year old, and Jeff, my two-year old, were launching into one of their regular battles. The shouting and crying went on for at least a minute, but by the time I got off the phone and into the living room, they were playing happily with their coloring books.

"All right," I demanded, "what's going on out here?"

Megan looked up with a serene smile and said, "It's okay, Mommie. We did peacemaking."

More suspicious than ever, I asked her to explain what had happened. "Well," she said, "I took Jeffrey's coloring book, and he started to hit me. So I hit him. Then he screamed, and I screamed. But then I said, 'Jeffrey, let's not fight. I'm sorry I took your book. Will you forgive me?' And he said, 'I 'give you, Megan. I sorry I hit you. 'Give me?' And I said, 'I forgive you,' and then we hugged and were friends again."

All I could do was drop to my knees, pull my children into my arms, and breathe a prayer of thanks to God. They were really learning how to be peacemakers! The principles I had been repeating to them for months on end were actually taking root. Yes, they fought again within the hour, but at least they were learning the basic principles they need to resolve their frequent differences in a constructive way.

That incident provided the final push I needed to pull this manual together. As a former school teacher and counselor, I had witnessed countless disputes in the classroom, on the playground, and in my students' homes. I had also seen how effective God's peacemaking principles could be in each setting, whether the students were in elementary school, junior high, or high school.

For example, one student learned to confess to stealing from a teacher and offered double restitution. Another student took responsibility for assaulting a principal and willingly accepted the resulting discipline. A third appealed successfully to her divorced parents to change a painful custody arrangement. And an entire class pulled together to forgive a rude and disruptive classmate and help him to develop better relationships.

Like dozens of others, these students learned to respond to conflict in a biblical manner. But for me the acid test was whether I could teach these principles to my own children. Although they, like their mother, are still not entirely consistent in this area, a positive pattern is definitely developing. Little by little they are learning to put off their natural reactions to conflict and replace them with responses that promote peace and reconciliation. If they can do it, so can the children in your home or classroom. I offer you this material to speed that process.

Before you invest your time and energy in this material, you have a right to know the basic convictions that guided my writing. First, I believe that God's Word is totally reliable and amazingly practical. Thus, when the Bible commands our children and us to live at peace with others, it also provides detailed and concrete guidance on how to carry out that sometimes difficult task.

Second, I believe that conflict is not necessarily wrong or destructive. If we teach our children to respond to it in a biblically faithful manner, conflict can become an opportunity for them to please and honor God, to serve other people, and to grow to be like Christ.

Third, I believe that many of the conflicts students experience are caused or aggravated by sin. Like adults, children wrestle with strong desires that sometimes get out of hand. We can and should use appropriate discipline to help them learn self-control and proper outward behavior. But it is even more important that we help them understand the root causes of their conflicts (pride, selfishness, greed, unforgiveness, etc.) and encourage them to ask God to free them from these sinful attitudes. Since Christ alone can offer such freedom, the gospel is an essential part of true peacemaking.

Fourth, I believe that the most important skills of a peacemaker are repentance, confession, and forgiveness. As important as communication and problem-solving skills are, they cannot heal relationships that have been damaged by conflict. True reconciliation comes only when students take responsibility for their wrongs, express sorrow for hurting others, and commit themselves to forgive one another as God has forgiven them.

I pray that this manual will help you to develop similar convictions and instill them in your students. Along the way you can help them to gain accurate insights into important peacemaking questions, such as:

- **What is at the heart of conflict?**

- **Is it possible to honor God in conflict?**

- **How can I take responsibility for my contribution to a conflict?**

- **How can I go and talk to someone if we are in a fight?**

- **How can we be friends again if there's a wall between us now?**

If you would like additional help in understanding God's answers to these questions, I encourage you to read *The Peacemaker: A Biblical Guide to Resolving Personal Conflict* (Baker Books, 2d ed. 1997), which was written by my husband, Ken Sande. Through his book you can learn even more about biblical conflict resolution and discover ways to be a positive example to your students. As you encourage and show one another how to be peacemakers, your home or classroom can increasingly become a place of peace.

May God guide you in your instruction and grant you and your students the blessings he has promised to peacemakers!

— Corlette Sande

> **The most important skills of a peacemaker are repentance, confession, and forgiveness.**

9

The Parent/Teacher Manual
Each lesson in the manual is divided into

6 lesson sections:

1. Setting the Stage:
This section includes an introduction to the lesson, a review of previous concepts, thought-provoking discussion questions, and a short story to illustrate the principles in the lesson. (A cartoon version of the stories is included in the Student Activity Sheets for students' use.)

2. The Lesson:
The lesson contains biblical principles of peacemaking needed to build the foundation for settling differences with others. If you teach all of the information in each lesson you will have accomplished the goals and objectives for that lesson. This section also includes optional role plays to reinforce these peacemaking principles.

3. Wrapping It Up:
This section includes an encouraging summary of the lesson's principles and a closing prayer.

4. Activities and Personal Application:
Each lesson has activities that are designed to help students apply the principles they have learned. Assign as many of these activities as you believe are appropriate to reinforce the information. These activities are available in a set of twelve comic book style Student Activity Booklets, which are reproducible (see page 6, Permission to Reproduce). There is one ten-page booklet for each of the twelve chapters.

5. Dig into the Word:
You will find a list of relevant Bible passages and applicable Bible stories at the end of each lesson. These passages reinforce the biblical foundation for the lesson.

6. Lesson Summary:
This section includes the Bible memory verse, the key principle, and a summary of the main points of the lesson.

2 The Student Activity Books

The Student Activity Books are divided into

4 sections:

1. Story:

A cartoon version of the story from each lesson is provided in the Student Activity Sheets. Students can refer to the cartoon as you read or tell the story.

2. Diagrams:

Diagrams are included to visually reinforce key points.

3. Resolution:

The conflict described in each story comes to a constructive conclusion.

4. Activities and Personal Application:

Assign as many of these activities as you need to reinforce the essential concepts of each lesson.

Goals of the Program

Immediate Goal:

With God's help, students will learn how to resolve personal conflicts in a biblically faithful manner and to enjoy the freedom of restored relationships.

Students will learn the importance of personal responsibility as it relates to conflict, and will discover ways to prevent conflict in the future. Students will learn that the Bible has the answers to their personal conflicts: repentance, confession, and forgiveness. They will begin to understand that they need to obey God regardless of how they feel.

Long Term Goal:

With God's help, students will develop a godly character and live as God's forgiven and sanctified people.

Students will learn skills that will strengthen their relationships with their families and friends. By learning how to use God's way of resolving conflicts, students will be better prepared to mature into responsible adults and experience more stable relationships at home, in the workplace, and in their communities. In addition, students can learn skills that can keep them from painful and unnecessary conflict as adults.

Twelve Key Principles for Young Peacemakers

1. Conflict is a slippery slope.
2. Conflict starts in the heart.
3. Choices have consequences.
4. Wise-way choices are better than my-way choices.
5. The blame game makes conflict worse.
6. Conflict is an opportunity.
7. The 5A's can resolve conflict.
8. Forgiveness is a choice.
9. It's never too late to start doing what's right.
10. Think before you speak.
11. Respectful communication is more likely to be heard.
12. A respectful appeal can prevent conflict.

This curriculum is designed to be used to teach intermediate and middle school students. Even so, the principles from *The Young Peacemaker* have been successfully taught to preschool students as well as high school students. You would need to adapt the stories and the language to teach younger or older students. Peacemaker Ministries intends to develop resources in the future that can be used to teach primary and secondary level students.

Christian Schools and Home Schools

There are twelve chapters in this manual. I recommend that teachers cover one chapter per week, using one or more sessions of twenty to forty minutes, depending on the age and attention span of the students. Teachers may teach more than one chapter per week if they wish to cover the material more quickly, or they may take more than one week to reinforce certain principles in some of the chapters.

Although each chapter could be taught in one session, teachers may wish to divide the chapters into smaller teaching sections for use throughout the week.

Use the Student Activity Books during class or as homework assignments to reinforce each lesson's principles.

Sunday Schools

There is more information in each lesson than Sunday school teachers will be able to cover during a single weekly Sunday school class. Teachers will need to thoroughly study each lesson and choose to teach those concepts that are most relevant to their students.

Some of the activities and worksheets in the Student Activity Books could be used during class times or as homework assignments to reinforce peacemaking principles.

Family Devotions

This material can also be used as a family devotional. Read and discuss as much information as you can during a thirty-minute devotional time. Use the role plays to reinforce the concepts you have taught. Encourage your children to memorize the key Bible verse for each lesson. Share appropriate examples of your personal struggle to be a peacemaker according to God's Word. In addition, explain how God has worked to help you be faithful and obedient to him as you respond to conflict situations.

Teaching Tips

The Peacemaker

One of the best ways to prepare for teaching the material in this manual is to read *The Peacemaker: A Biblical Guide to Resolving Personal Conflict* by Ken Sande (Baker Books, 2d ed. 1997). *The Young Peacemaker* is a simplified version of this book.

Learning the Material

I strongly recommend that you read the entire manual before you begin to teach your students. You may wish to teach the lessons in a different order than the one presented. Please feel free to do so. Flexibility and meeting your students' needs are most important.

Talking

Lively discussion is an important part of this course. Please make it your habit to invite appropriate student responses to questions throughout all the lessons. While there will be some questions that have right or wrong answers, many discussion questions can be answered with a variety of responses. Students should be encouraged to express their ideas. Always speak respectfully to your students as you respond to their answers. Your example will be an excellent teaching tool. Remember to reinforce correct or thoughtful answers with praise.

Creative Answers

If answers are wrong or contradictory to Scripture, this may be an indication that some principles need to be reviewed. You will find examples of appropriate answers in parentheses after most questions. If students give unrealistic or attention-getting answers, simply acknowledge the answer by saying something like, "That's a thought. I'm certainly glad that doesn't usually happen." It is important not to argue with the students as to whether their answers are good or bad. Arguing is not a good example and could create a conflict. If necessary you may want to speak with a student privately about an inappropriate answer or a confusing concept.

Parental Cooperation

Parent and teacher cooperation is of utmost importance if this program is to benefit families and schools. In Appendix B you will find a letter to parents that explains how parents can support *The Young Peacemaker* program. Encourage students to take all of their activity sheets home each week and review them with their parents. If possible, schedule a meeting for parents and teachers to explain the program and address questions. An audio tape that provides an overview of the program is available from Peacemaker Ministries.

Tools of the Trade

Use a blackboard, overhead projector, or charts for visual reinforcement.

You may need to define some words. The vocabulary may stretch some students.

Know and teach from Proverbs! Barbara Decker has developed a very helpful and well organized resource called *Proverbs for Parenting* (Pub. 1991, Lynn's Bookshelf, PO Box 2224, Boise, ID 83701). I highly recommend this resource for your parenting library.

You may need to explain some Bible verses or stories to students. For Bible stories, I recommend that you use a good children's Bible such as *The NIV Adventure Bible* (Zondervan, 1994) and *The NIV Young Discoverer's Bible* (Zondervan, 1985).

Know and teach from Proverbs!

The Peace Table

Set up a *Peace Table* or a *Problem Solving Corner* in your home or school room where students can go to resolve their conflicts after they have learned how to do so. When they come to tattle on each other, simply send them to the peace table to work out the problem. Then have them report back to you as to how they resolved the conflict.

Sharing Personal Experience

Make yourself vulnerable when you are teaching this material. Let the students know that you struggle in some of these areas, and that you are asking the Lord to help you to become a better peace-maker. As you share *appropriate personal examples* with your students, they can learn what to do and what not to do in conflict situations.

Consequences

As parents and teachers, we have an important task of teaching and training our students in righteousness and responsibility (Deut. 6:4-7). With that command in mind, I suggest that we take seriously the following thoughts:

Threats and promises are not consequences! When we tell our students that they will receive a discipline or a blessing, then we must follow through. Otherwise we teach them that consequences mean nothing. If we break our word to them we will not be setting a godly example!

There will be times when our students will need to be disciplined because of their choices. *When we rescue them from their deserved consequences, we are only promot-ing their childish behavior, immaturity, and irresponsibility.* It is more loving to allow them to accept their consequences so that they may become more responsible and self-disciplined in the future.

Ideally, students should make good choices simply because it is the right thing to do. However, *a carefully chosen consequence can motivate them to seek God's help so they can make the right choice more often.*

Carefully chosen and infrequent rewards could be used as good consequences for those who return homework assignments. Students need to see consequences in a positive light.

Use Every Opportunity
to Teach Peacemaking

"Hear, O Israel: The L ord our God, the Lord is one. L ove the L ord your God with all your heart and with all your soul and with all your strength. These commandments that I give to you today are to be upon your hearts. Impress them on your children. T alk about them when you sit at home and when you walk along the road, when you lie down and when you get up " (Deut. 6:4-7).

Talking:
Talk about peacemaking whenever the opportunity arises.

Use Pictures:
Use drawings, pictures, and stories that illustrate peacemaking principles. Involve the students in listing important concepts.

Role Plays:
Make up a story that involves a conflict and then assign roles to the students and yourself. Practice using effective conflict resolution skills. Evaluate each other's participation in the role play. How well did you communicate your thoughts and feelings? How well did you take responsibility for your actions? How many choices did you come up with to solve the problem? Always do this in a constructive manner.

Story Openers:
Read or make up story openers that the students finish by thinking of ways to solve the story's conflict. They could write an ending to the story and act it out for their friends, family, or classmates. Build on their creativity!

TV Examples:
Watch selected television programs with your students and identify the constructive or destructive ways of handling conflict, such as taking responsibility versus blaming. Watch for examples of proper or improper communication.

Bible Stories:
Read Bible stories about Joseph, Deborah, David, Daniel, Jesus, and Paul and discuss how God helped them to handle the conflicts they had with others.

Real Life:
Use students' actual experiences as teaching opportunities to discover better ways of responding to conflict.

Bible Memory:
Help students memorize relevant Scripture verses that they can use in making wise decisions and handling conflict biblically.

Your Example:
The *best way to teach peacemaking principles to students is to demonstrate them in your own life.* All adults (parents, family members, teachers) need to understand how their example will teach students either to aggravate conflict or to deal with it in a responsible way.

Part One
Understanding Conflict

Before children can learn how to settle arguments and fights, they need to understand what conflict is and how it grows. In this section you will teach your students to identify their typical responses to conflict, to discover what is at the heart of their conflicts, to see how their consequences are directly related to their choices, and to find a better way to make choices in the first place.

Lesson 1

Conflict Is a Slippery Slope

If it is possible, as far as it depends on you, **live at peace** with everyone.

Romans 12:18

Lesson Goal:

To help students understand what conflict is and how they can respond to it.

Lesson Objectives:

By God's grace students will learn:
1. What conflict is.
2. Different responses to conflict (the slippery slope diagram).
3. God is with them—even in conflict.

Key Principle:

Conflict is a slippery slope.

Lesson Needs:

Bible
Student Activity Book #1

Begin with Prayer

Begin the lesson with prayer for wisdom and faithfulness as children learn to apply God's Word in their lives. Pray that your students will understand what conflict is and learn to respond to it in a godly way.

Note to Teachers

Role plays can be threatening to children. Be sure to deal with any put-downs or ridicule promptly. You can help students feel secure during their role plays by letting them know that making fun of each other will not be tolerated.

Setting the Stage

Today we are going to begin to study conflict. According to Webster's Dictionary, the word conflict means: "a clash between hostile or opposing elements or ideas."

- **Can you simplify that definition?** (Conflict is a fight between people who think or act differently.)

- **Can anyone tell me some other names for conflict?** (Fights, quarrels, disagreements, arguments.)

- **How many of you have ever been involved in a conflict? Briefly explain what happened.** (Encourage some students to share a few of their personal experiences.)

- **How do you feel when you are in conflict with someone?** (Angry, hurt, sad, frustrated, lonely.)

- **With whom can people have conflicts?** (Parents, brothers, sisters, other family members, teachers, friends, police, store clerks.)

- **What happens to relationships when people get into a conflict?**

- **How do people feel and act when they are in a conflict?**

When you are in conflict with others, you are usually not very happy. Conflict can bring out the worst in you, and you may say or do things that will make the conflict worse.

Starting today you are going to learn some important information about conflict.

- You will learn to recognize the difference between good and bad conflict.
- You will learn how to resolve and prevent bad conflict.
- You will learn how to have better relationships with other people.

Twisted Ten Speed

featuring
KENT & JAMES

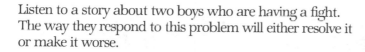

> WHAT HAPPENED TO MY NEW BIKE?

Listen to a story about two boys who are having a fight. The way they respond to this problem will either resolve it or make it worse.

Kent couldn't wait to show James his new mountain bike. He was so proud of it—he had saved for two years to get enough money to buy just the one he wanted. As he saw his best friend James walking up the sidewalk, Kent hopped on his new bike and rode down the sidewalk to meet him.

James couldn't believe his eyes! "Wow! What a cool bike, Kent! So this is why you wouldn't spend any extra money."

Kent returned the grin and said, "Now that I have a bike like yours we can ride everywhere together. Let's start by riding back to school. I forgot to bring home my jacket this afternoon."

"YES!" James replied enthusiastically.

When they got to school, they left their bikes at the end of the parking lot. While Kent went inside to get his jacket, he assumed that James would watch the bikes. While James was waiting for him, he heard some kids playing basketball, so he went around the corner to see the game. A few minutes later he heard Kent scream. James went running back to where they had left their bikes in the parking lot. Kent's bike was lying on the ground all bent and twisted.

"My new bike!!!" Kent yelled. "What happened to my bike, James?"

"I don't know what happened. I was only gone for a minute," replied James, stunned.

"Someone smashed it to pieces, that's what happened. And it's your fault. You should have been watching it."

"Listen! It's not my fault!" James fired back. "I can't help it if somebody wrecked your bike. It's not fair to blame me for this!"

"Well, all I know is I left my bike with you and now it's all bent and scratched up. I want it replaced, so you'd better figure out how to come up with the money to get me a new bike!" With that, Kent stormed away, leaving behind a confused and angry James.

Kent and James are learning that **conflict is a slippery slope.** If they are not careful, they could slide into a danger zone by running away from the conflict or by attacking each other. This will only make the conflict worse and possibly do permanent damage to their relationship. Only by staying on top of the slippery slope will they be able to solve the conflict and preserve their friendship.

21

The SLIPPERY SLOPE

Let's look carefully at this slippery slope diagram and see the nine ways people can respond to conflict.

The slippery slope is divided into three sections. Two sections are "danger zones."

The escape responses are used to get away from conflict instead of trying to resolve it. They often prolong conflict and can result in bitterness and unforgiveness.

Denial

Pretending that a conflict does not exist, or refusing to do what we can to work it out, is always a wrong response to conflict.

■ **What do you think might happen if Kent or James denied that there was a problem?**

Kent chooses to say nothing to James about his bike getting bent and scratched. Because he says nothing, he probably gets angrier and angrier. Even if he pretends that nothing is wrong, he still sends unspoken messages to James that he is upset. Or James acts like the "bike thing" was not a big deal. He clowns around about it, and eventually refuses to talk about it.

Blame Game

Instead of taking responsibility for our choices, we try to escape their consequences by blaming others for the problem, pretending we did nothing wrong, covering up what we did, or lying about our contribution to a conflict. This is never a responsible way to handle conflict, nor does it resolve problems.

■ **How would the choice to blame**

someone else affect the boys' relationship?

Once Kent confronts James about his wrecked bike, James makes excuses for not taking care of his friend's bike or blames someone else for the problem. James claims it is Kent's fault the bike was damaged because he left the bike at the end of the parking lot in the first place.

Run Away

Running away from the person we are quarreling with is only acceptable if there is danger of harm. Otherwise this response does not solve problems.

■ **How would the choice to run away from the problem affect Kent and James' friendship?**

Both boys might start avoiding each other, refusing to talk or even look at each other.

The escape responses may be referred to as *peace-faking* because we try to pretend there is peace between us and the other person when there really isn't. None of the escape responses will solve the dispute over Kent's bike.

Role Play Activity: Have two students act out what it would look like if Kent and James used the escape response to resolve their conflict.

The attack responses are used to put pressure on others to get our own way. These responses usually damage relationships and often result in anger and hatred.

Put Downs

We attack others with harsh and cruel words when conflict arises. This response usually stirs up anger in the other person, and is always a wrong response to conflict.

- **What would the choice to put each other down do to Kent and James' friendship and their conflict?**

The boys start mocking one another by saying hurtful and unkind things to each other. This could destroy their friendship.

Gossip

We talk about people behind their backs in order to damage their reputation or to get others on our side. Gossip is hurtful and is always a wrong response to a conflict.

- **Who else could this response affect besides Kent and James? How?**

Kent and James start saying mean things about each other to their classmates and friends.

Fight

We use physical force to get our own way. This is almost always a wrong response to conflict. (This response is proper only if you have to protect yourself or another person from being injured by an attacker.)

- **What might happen to Kent and James if they choose to fight about the bike?**

Kent and James get into a fist fight and start calling each other names. Both boys could get hurt physically.

The attack responses may be referred to as *peace-breaking* because we break apart our relationship with others by verbal and physical attacks against one another.

Role Play Activity: Have the students act out what it would look like if Kent and James used the attack responses in their situation.

Optional Topics for Discussion

Note to Teachers

There are three extreme responses to conflict that you may choose to discuss with some children. They are not shown on the slippery slope diagram.

Suicide

is the most extreme **escape** response (below "run away"). Sometimes people think taking their own lives is the only solution to their problems. They need to understand that their problems are usually temporary. But suicide is forever—it doesn't solve any problems!

Litigation

is another **attack** response (between "gossip" and "fight"). Some people will attack their opponent by suing that person in a court of law. Some lawsuits are necessary, but most conflict that results in a lawsuit could be handled more constructively by staying on top of the slippery slope diagram.

Murder

is the most extreme **attack** response (below "fight"). Some people will even kill those who stand in their way or who make them angry. Murder is always a wrong response to conflict.

Work-It-Out

None of the escape or attack responses will resolve the conflict between Kent and James. In fact, those responses will only make the conflict worse. But there is a way that Kent and James can "stay on top of conflict" by using the work-it-out responses.

The work-it-out responses are found at the top of the curve. These responses usually lead to constructive solutions to conflicts and help to preserve relationships. They are carried out in three different ways.

The first two ways can be done personally and privately.

Overlook an Offense

You deal with the offense *by yourself*. You simply *decide to forgive* a wrong action against you and walk away from a conflict. Perhaps you think this is the same as denial, but forgiveness is the key here. The person who overlooks another's offenses will continue to have a growing, healthy relationship with him or her. "Don't sweat the small stuff!" (see Prov. 12:16; 17:14; 19:11; Col. 3:13; 1 Peter 4:8)

■ **What would it look like if Kent overlooked this problem? Is this a problem that should be overlooked? Why?**

After the blowup, Kent cools down and begins to think of how he can stay on top of this problem. He remembers that one of his options is to overlook the offense. He decides against this option because his bike is damaged and he needs to find out what really happened. In addition, the two friends already said some harsh words to each other that will damage their friendship if they don't work it out. (Since he cannot overlook the problem, Kent should use one of the following work-it-out responses.)

Talk-It-Out

A conflict is resolved by going directly to the other person to *talk it out together*. This can include confessing your own wrongs and confronting the other person's wrongs in a kind and respectful way. This response should be used if you cannot overlook what the other person did, and the problem is hurting your relationship (see Matt. 5:23-24; 18:15; see also Prov. 28:13; Gal. 6:1-3).

■ **How could Kent and James talk together about their conflict?**

Kent walks over to where James is watching the basketball game and explains how he found his bike. He asks James if he knows what happened to the bike. Doing so will give James a chance to explain what he knows about the situation. This response gives the boys an

opportunity to work together to find out what happened to the bike.

If James doesn't know how the bike got damaged, Kent needs to know this so that he won't wrongfully accuse his friend. By working together, Kent and James might be able to find out who damaged the bike and help the person responsible to face the consequences of his or her actions.

If James hurriedly laid the bike down on the parking lot before running off to watch the game, then he should confess his carelessness to Kent. He should offer to get the bike fixed or replaced since his actions resulted in damage to the bike. If he sincerely confesses and is willing to make it right, then it will be easier for Kent to forgive him.

The third way to resolve a conflict is to get help from others.

Get Help to Know What You Should Say

When you are in a difficult conflict, it is often wise to ask someone else (such as a parent, teacher, or friend) to help you decide how you can handle the conflict so it won't get worse—at least from your side. This is called *coaching*. Ask the person to help you decide what you should say and how you should say it (see Prov. 15:1; Eph. 4:29).

If the boys' attempts to solve their prob-

lem do not work, then one or both of them may ask someone they trust (like their parents, a teacher, a pastor, or a mature friend) to help them talk it out. It's important to realize that both boys have a responsibility to work on the conflict. However, either one of the boys could ask someone to coach him to make choices that could solve the problem.

Get Help to Talk Together

When you cannot resolve the conflict just between the two of you, then ask someone else to meet with both of you to help you talk together and find a solution to the problem. This is called *mediation*. Mediators only suggest solutions—you still need to decide what to do (see Matt. 18:16).

If the boys' attempts to talk it out continue to be unsuccessful and they see that they are heading down the slippery slope (either by escaping the problem or attacking each other), they could agree to ask someone they trust to meet with them and help them work out their differences.

Get Help to Decide

If you cannot solve a conflict by talking with each other or by mediation, then you can both tell your side of the story to a person in authority who will decide on a solution. This is called *arbitration*. The helping person (an arbitrator) could be a parent, teacher, school administrator,

or pastor (see 1 Cor. 6:1-8; Exod. 18:13-27).

If coaching and mediation do not work, the boys could ask someone in authority (probably their parents) to listen to both sides of the story and then decide what should be done.

The work-it-out responses may be referred to as *peace-making* because we try to bring peace back into the relationship by our efforts to confess and confront it in a respectful way.

If Kent and James use the work-it-out process to resolve the bike problem, they will stay on top of the slippery slope and resolve the conflict in a constructive way. They will feel confident that the problem will be solved, and they will keep their friendship strong and healthy.

Whatever work-it-out response the boys choose, they would be wise to involve their parents in the process. Their parents will trust and respect their children for learning to solve problems responsibly.

> **Role Play Activity:** Have two students act out the work-it-out responses to Kent and James' conflict about the damaged bike.

CONFLICT IS A SLIPPERY SLOPE.

God Is with You—
Even in Conflict

As you study the concepts in this course remember that when you are in a conflict God is always with you, and he will help you stay on top of the slippery slope. Because he is with you, you can be confident that conflict is an opportunity to do good things. In particular, you can please God, grow to be like Christ, and serve other people—both those involved in the conflict and those watching how you handle it. Let's look at two Bible stories that show God is always with his people—even in a conflict.

Teaching Tip

Read the following Bible stories to your children and discuss them. These stories will help children understand that God is with his people in difficult situations.

Daniel's Diet

Read Daniel 1:1-21. (Daniel appeals to the king's guard to be allowed to eat a more healthy diet.)

Daniel chose to glorify God by showing respect to the king's officials. Instead of refusing to obey the king's requirement to eat only the royal food, he respectfully asked for permission to be tested. He said, "Please test your servants for ten days: Give us nothing but vegetables to eat and water to drink. Then compare our appearance with that of the young men who eat the royal food, and treat your servants in accordance with what you see" (Daniel 1:12-13). The guard agreed, and at the end of the ten days Daniel and his friends looked healthier and better nourished than the young men who ate the royal food. Daniel could have chosen to defy the king and refuse to cooperate with his officials, or he could have eaten the food and disobeyed God. Both of these responses would have created serious problems for Daniel and the other Israelites. Instead, Daniel chose to glorify God by humbly relying on God's wisdom to find a way to eat a more healthy diet. Daniel knew what God wanted him to do, and God helped him work with his opponent to accomplish faithful obedience. *God was with Daniel and his friends!*

The Lions' Night

Read Daniel 6:1-28. (Daniel is thrown into the lions' den for his faithful obedience to God.)

Daniel continued to earn favor with the kings of Babylon because of his wisdom and faithful service. When King Darius took over the kingdom, he planned to give Daniel a place of honor. The king's officials did not want to be under Daniel's authority, so they laid a trap for him. They persuaded the king to sign a law requiring that any person who prayed to anyone but the king would be thrown into the lions' den. Daniel could have obeyed the king's law, but he chose to remain faithful to God. He knew that God's law was higher than human law, so he continued to pray faithfully to God as he always did. Consequently, he was thrown into a den of lions. But God protected him and the next day King Darius found Daniel alive. "Daniel, servant of the living God, has your God, whom you serve continually, been able to rescue you from the lions?" Daniel answered, "O king, live forever! My God sent his angel, and he shut the mouths of the lions. They have not hurt me, because I was found innocent in his sight. Nor have I ever done any wrong before you, O king" (Daniel 6:20-22). The king was so amazed by Daniel's God that he sent a decree to his people: "I issue a decree that in every part of my kingdom people must fear and reverence the God of Daniel" (Daniel 6:26). *God was with Daniel, and Daniel glorified God!*

These stories show that our God is a personal and loving God, and he is always with you. At times he will immediately deliver you from a difficult situation, as he did in the first story about Daniel. But, as you learned from the second story, sometimes God will take you through a conflict to teach you to love and trust him more.

What Can Be Good about Conflict?

Many people think that all conflict is bad. Often they will try to escape or attack at the first sign of a conflict. Actually conflict provides an opportunity for us to do what is right and please God (not ourselves) by responding in the ways that the Bible teaches. You are going to learn in this course how to handle relationship problems more constructively instead of falling off the slippery slope into bad ways of responding to conflict.

Wrapping It Up

You learned that a conflict is a fight between people who think and act differently. You also learned that **conflict is a slippery slope.** If you are not careful, you can slide into the escape or attack zone, which will usually make conflict worse and damage relationships. Instead of sliding off the edge of the slippery slope, you can learn to handle your fights and quarrels in a constructive way by staying in the work-it-out zone. There are times to overlook the problem, while at other times you may need to go in private to talk together. If that doesn't work, you can get help from others through coaching, mediation, or arbitration. During the next few weeks you are going to learn about ways that you can choose to stay on top of conflict. You will talk about where conflict comes from, how to respond to it properly, and how to try to prevent it when you can. You are going to learn how to be peacemakers for Jesus!

Closing Prayer

Dear Lord, I have a lot to learn about conflict and how to handle it better. Most of the time I respond by escaping or attacking. I can see now that those responses make my conflicts worse and even hurt my relationships with others. Teach me how to be a peacemaker, Lord. In Jesus' name,

Amen.

Making It Real

Assign one or more of the suggested activities for Lesson One that are found in the Activities and Personal Application section of this lesson. Some of the activities are included in Student Activity Book #1.

Activities and Personal Application

Activities one and two can be found in Student Activity Book (SAB) #1.

1. Can You Survive the Slippery Slope? (see SAB 1-9): Using the slippery slope diagram as a guide, identify the ways you usually respond to conflict.

2. Bible Heroes on the Slippery Slope (see SAB 1-10): Indicate which slippery slope response was used in each situation. (This activity is best done as a group activity. The answers are given below.)

Adam and Eve are confronted with their sin (Gen. 3:8-13). *(blame game)*

Cain murders Abel (Gen. 4:2b-8). *(fight)*

Eli denies the seriousness of his sons' sin (1 Sam. 2:22-25). *(denial)*

David fights with Goliath (1 Sam. 17:1-51). *(fight-good)*

Nathan confronts David about his adultery and murder (2 Sam. 11:1-12:13). *(talk it out)*

Jonah runs away from God (Jonah 1:1-3:3). *(run away)*

Daniel wants to eat proper foods (Dan. 1:8-16). *(talk it out)*

Joseph flees with Mary and Jesus to Egypt (Matt. 2:13-15). *(run away-good)*

The Christians argue about how to distribute food (Acts 6:1-7). *(get help through mediation)*

People do not want to hear Stephen talk about Jesus (Acts 6:8-15; 7:54-60). *(put downs, gossip, fight)*

People criticize Peter for preaching to the Gentiles (Acts 11:1-18). *(talk it out)*

The Christians have a doctrinal dispute (Acts 15:1-32). *(get help through arbitration)*

The Philippians oppose Paul's ministry (Acts 16:16-22). *(put downs, gossip, fight)*

The Ephesians oppose Paul's ministry (Acts 19:23-41). *(put downs, gossip, fight; finally resolved by getting help)*

3. Watch a video or television program or read a book with your family and write a description of how the story characters handle conflict in terms of the slippery slope diagram.

Dig into the Word

Memory Verse:

Romans 12:18

Other Relevant Bible Verses:

Proverbs 12:16, 17:14, 19:11, 29:13
Matthew 5:23-24, 18:15-20
1 Corinthians 6:1-8
Galatians 6:1-3
Colossians 3:13
1 Peter 4:8

Applicable Bible Stories:

Assign one or more of the passages given in activity two (Bible Heroes on the Slippery Slope) to help children analyze conflict situations in the Bible.

The Lesson Summary

Bible Memory Verse:
"If it is possible, as far as it depends on you, live at peace with everyone" (Rom. 12:18).

Key Principle:
Conflict is a slippery slope.

The Main Points of the Lesson

1. What is conflict?

A clash between hostile or opposing elements or ideas.

A fight between people who think or act differently.

Fights, quarrels, arguments and disagreements are other names for conflict.

2. Different responses to conflict (The slippery slope diagram)

The Escape Responses

- Denial: Pretend a conflict doesn't exist.
- Blame game: Place responsibility for conflict on others.
- Run away: Run away from the reality of the conflict.

The Attack Responses

- Put downs: Say hurtful or threatening things to someone.
- Gossip: Talk behind a person's back to damage his reputation.
- Fight: Use physical force to get what you want.

The Work-It-Out Responses

- Overlook: Decide to forgive and walk away from a conflict.
- Talk: Confess your sinful choices and confront in a kind way.
- Get help: Coaching, mediation, or arbitration can help you resolve conflict.

3. God is with you even in conflict

Conflict provides an opportunity to please God (not ourselves) by responding in ways the Bible teaches.

Lesson 2 — What Causes Conflict?

What
causes fights
and quarrels
among you?
Don't
they come
from your
**desires
that battle
within
you?**
You want
something
but don't
get it.

James 4:1-2

Lesson Goal:

To help children understand what causes conflict.

Lesson Objectives:

By God's grace children will learn:
1. Where conflict comes from.
2. What causes conflict.
3. That there are some good reasons for conflict.

Key Principle:

Conflict starts in the heart.

Lesson Needs:

Bible
Student Activity Book #2
Worksheet One—Identifying Good and
 Bad Choices (Appendix C)

Begin with Prayer

Begin with a prayer that your students will learn to recognize what is at the heart of their conflicts and that God will fill their hearts with a desire to please and honor him.

If time permits, discuss one or more of the assigned activities from the previous lesson as a review. Collect and evaluate any assignments that are not discussed in class, and return them to the students with your comments so they can see that doing their homework is worthwhile.

Review and Setting the Stage

- **Do you remember the three types of responses to conflict on the slippery slope?** (Escape, attack, or work-it-out.)

- **What are the escape responses?** (Denial, blame game, run away.)

- **What are the attack responses?** (Put downs, gossip, fight.)

- **What are the work-it-out responses?** (Overlook, talk, get help.)

- **According to the slippery slope, how have you responded to conflict this week?** (Encourage brief responses.)

Star Runner Stormed Out

featuring TONY & HIS MOM

In today's lesson we will discuss some facts about choices and their relationship to conflict. We will learn that **conflict starts in the heart**. First, listen to a story about a family that is involved in a conflict.

Tony and his friend, Eric, could hardly wait to see the premier showing of the new blockbuster movie, Star Runner III. Star Runner movies were their all-time favorites, and they had been waiting months for this one to be released. Tony was getting ready to leave when his mother came into his room. "Tony," she said, "I just heard on the radio that there's a severe storm warning for our area, so I don't want you to go out this afternoon. You and Eric will have to make plans to go to the movie another time!"

"Mom! You can't be serious! It's the pre-mier showing of Star Runner III! Eric and I have seen the premier showings of Star Runner I and II! We just can't miss this one! Please, Mom," pleaded Tony.

"I'm sorry, Tony, I don't want you out when there's a dangerous storm coming! You'll just have to see it another time."

Tony stormed out of the room and slammed the door. "You never let me have any fun!" he yelled.

"You come back here this minute, young man! You'd better not talk to me that way," screamed his mother.

■ **Where does Tony's response fit on the slippery slope?** (The attack response: Tony yelled at his mother; and the escape response: Tony ran away from the conflict by storming off to his room.)

The conflict between Tony and his mother started in their hearts. Tony's heart was set on seeing the movie with his friend, and his mother's desire was for her son to accept her decision respectfully. Today we'll discuss how **conflict starts in the heart.**

Conflict Starts in the Heart

Our choices come from our hearts. If our hearts are filled with selfish desires, we will often make choices that lead to conflict. But if our hearts are filled with a desire to love and please God, we will usually make choices that promote peace.

Where Conflict Comes From

God wants you to know that **conflict starts in the heart**. Many of our conflicts happen because we want our own way and make choices to get it. The Bible talks about our selfish desires as the reason for many of our conflicts.

"What causes fights and quarrels among you? Don't they come from your desires that battle within you? You want something but don't get it" (James 4:1-2).

Our selfish desires are at the root of many of our fights with other people. Sinful, self-serving desires often take control of our hearts. The heart is like a battlefield where our selfish desires are at war with what we know is right. Our desires can fool us. We will often think that our selfish desires are right, but if they lead us to disobey God's Word, they are wrong! When we give in to them, we often end up in a conflict with someone. Here are some examples of times when you could find yourself in a conflict if you let your selfish desires rule over you:

- You want to stay up longer, but your parents say you need to go to bed.
- You want to go swimming, but your friend wants to go bike riding.
- You want to go outside to play, but your teacher says you must stay in to do your work.

■ **Can you think of other examples of desires that can cause conflict?** (Teachers, remember to reinforce appropriate answers.)

Root Desires that Can Lead to Sinful Choices

Plants get their nourishment through their roots. If those roots are good, a plant will produce good fruit. Likewise, bad roots will produce bad fruit (see Luke 6:43-45). Like plants, we have a root system in our hearts that produces different kinds of fruit. This root system is made up of the desires that are in our hearts. The fruit that grows from these roots is all the choices we make to say and do things. If our hearts are filled with selfish desires, the fruit will usually be sinful words and actions that result in conflict and broken relationships. On the other hand, if our hearts are filled with love for God and a desire to please him, then the fruit will be words and actions that promote peace and strengthen relationships.

Some of the desires in our hearts are clearly wrong, like greed or selfishness, and will produce bad fruit. Other desires may seem to be good, like wanting to get good grades, but even a good desire can produce bad fruit if you desire something too much. The desire can become a sinful demand. When you demand your own way, you are likely to offend others. This is how conflict often begins (see James 4:1-2).

Teaching Tip

I strongly suggest that you read *Shepherding a Child's Heart* by Tedd Tripp (Shepherd Press, 1995) for insights into this important subject.

Root: You think you are better than others. You don't like to be wrong.

Fruit: You become defensive and argumentative when someone corrects you.

Root: You want your own way.

Fruit: You will argue, nag, whine, lie, or throw a temper tantrum to try to get people to give in to your desires.

Root: You want more, and you are not content with what you have.

Fruit: You complain that you don't have what other people have. You take things that don't belong to you.

Root: You are afraid of what others will think of you. You want too much to be liked and accepted. You want other people to approve of you and applaud your efforts.

Fruit: You won't tell your friends that you are a Christian because you are afraid that they will think you are strange and reject you. You go along with your friends, even when you know that what they are doing is wrong, so that they will accept you. You need constant reassurance that you are doing well.

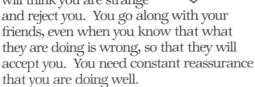

Root: You feel sorry for yourself and you want others to feel sorry for you, too.

Fruit: You pout and say, "Nobody has as many chores to do as me!" or "You never let me do anything!" or "Nobody likes me!"

Root: You want what others have. You are not content with what you have.

Fruit: If your sister gets a new shirt, then you want one as well. You make fun of your brother because he gets good grades and yours aren't as good.

Root: You don't want to work. You resist responsibility.

Fruit: You refuse to do your chores or schoolwork. You sit and watch TV instead of doing something constructive.

Root: You are afraid of losing the love or friendship of someone special if that person pays attention to someone else.

Fruit: You become angry at your friend for inviting another friend to go skating. You try to do everything you can to break up their friendship.

■ **What do you think could have been some of the root causes of the conflict between Tony and his mother?** (Tony: Selfishness or wanting his own way; fear of what Eric would think if Tony said he couldn't go. His mother: A desire to be in control without being questioned. A parent's goal to be obeyed and respected is biblical, but treating a child disrespectfully by screaming is sinful.)

■ **What is usually the root desire of your choices?** (Answers will vary.)

If you allow your selfish desires to control you, you will often make wrong choices, and your life may be filled with conflict.

That is bad news, isn't it?

A Heart that Desires to Love and Please God

The good news is that you do not have to be controlled by sinful desires! You can ask the Lord to forgive you for following your selfish desires. More importantly, you can ask him to replace those sinful desires with the very best desire of all: to love him with all your heart and to please him in everything you do. As God changes your heart and gives you the desire to love and please him, you will be able to say no to your selfish desires and make the kind of good choices that lead to peace. This is the kind of fruit that God loves to produce in our lives through his Holy Spirit (see Gal. 5:22-23).

Let's look at the fruit that comes from a heart that desires to love and please God.

Root: The desire to love and please God.

Fruit—Love: A loving heart shows an unselfish concern for others and desires to do good to them. For example, you will choose to play a game with your friend, even if you don't particularly enjoy it, because you know it is your friend's favorite game.

Fruit—Patience: A patient heart will wait without grumbling or complaining. For example, you will choose to wait your turn instead of demanding to go first. You will patiently wait for someone to give you something you have asked for.

Fruit—Kindness: A kind heart is interested in the well-being of others and will be considerate and helpful toward them. For example, you will choose to befriend someone who is seen as different instead of ridiculing the person as others do. You will treat others as you want them to treat you.

Fruit—Gentleness: A gentle heart is compassionate toward others. It is kind and loving, not harsh or violent. For example, you will speak with a gentle voice to someone who speaks angrily to you. As Proverbs 15:1 says: "A gentle answer turns away wrath, but a harsh word stirs up anger."

Teaching Tip

Remind your students that the only way to have hearts that please God is to ask him to change their hearts so they will love him and desire to please him more than to please themselves (Psalm 37:4-6).

At the root and in the heart is a desire to love and please God. (Gal. 5:22-23)

39

What Causes Conflict?

As we have seen, Tony and his mother had desires that ruled their hearts. Tony wanted to go the movie and his mother wanted to be obeyed. Neither desire was wrong until they made the choice to argue and get angry with each other when their desires weren't satisfied.

Careless Accidents

While some conflicts are caused by accidents, most are caused by choices. Both accidents and choices involve something that people do or say. Many people call choices they make "accidents." For instance, Tony might say, "Sure I stomped off and the door slammed, but it was an accident."

■ **Was it really an accident that Tony stomped off and slammed the door?** (No. It was a deliberate choice.)

Let's look at the difference between choices and accidents. People do not have accidents on purpose. Accidents are usually the result of carelessness. For example, it is usually an accident when you:

● Bump into someone you didn't see.
● Spill a glass of milk on the counter as you reach for the cereal.
● Fall down and tear your jeans.

An accident will not always cause a conflict between people, but a sinful or angry response to an accident can cause a conflict. If you yell and say hurtful things to your friend who accidentally knocked your books on the floor, then your response to the accident could cause a conflict.

Give an example of a better response to your friend's accident. (To pick up your books; to reassure your friend that you are not angry with her or him; to admit that you have done the same thing sometimes; to be understanding and forgiving.)

■ **Can you think of a right response to an accident that you caused?** (To apologize for what you did; to help clean up a mess you made; to do all you can to make your relationship right again.)

Deliberate Choices

Unlike accidents, choices are deliberate. In other words, choices result in our saying or doing something on purpose (or deliberately not saying or doing something). For example, it is a choice to:

● Hit your brother.
● Tell a lie.
● Take something that doesn't belong to you.

● Talk back to your parents.
● Call your friend a name.
● Not come home on time.
● Not do your work at home or at school.
● Not clean your room.
● Not tell the truth.

Your Choices Are Your Responsibility

Every choice is personal. Many times people blame others for their choices. But remember, choices are deliberate. Whether you make a choice after careful consideration or in the heat of the moment, each choice that you make belongs to you. Your choices are your responsibility. It is no one's fault but yours if you choose to say or do something that you know is wrong, causes conflict, or gets you into trouble.

■ **Whose fault was it that Tony stomped out of the room and slammed the door?** (It was Tony's fault. Even if his mother spoke sharply to him or he disagreed with her decision, Tony was one-hundred-percent responsible for his choices and actions.)

God's Word says that choices are stored up in our hearts. Let's read Luke 6:45 together.

"The good man brings good things out of the good stored up in his heart, and the evil man brings evil things out of the evil stored up in his heart. For out of the overflow of his heart his mouth speaks" (Luke 6:45).

Choices in Conflict

As you learned from the slippery slope diagram, you make choices about how you will respond to conflict. One way to handle conflict is to run away from it or pretend it isn't there (the escape response). Escape choices rarely resolve conflicts or build stronger relationships, so they are usually considered bad choices.

Another way to handle conflict is to attack others and try to hurt them (the attack response). Attack choices usually make conflict worse and are usually bad choices.

Another way to handle conflict is to overlook offenses, talk it out respectfully, or get help from others (the work-it-out responses). Work-it-out choices please

Good choices come from a heart that wants to please Jesus, while bad choices come from a heart intent on pleasing yourself. Throughout the Bible you find examples of these two types of choices. We'll talk more about this later in the lesson. For now, let's take a look at good and bad choices from God's point of view.

Good choices are:

- right
- obedient
- respectful
- wise
- righteous

Bad choices are:

- wrong
- disobedient
- disrespectful
- foolish
- sinful

■ **Can you name some specific examples of good and bad choices that kids make?**

God and usually speed up the problem-solving and reconciliation process. They are good choices.

Let's take a closer look at some good and bad choices in conflict. Choices are bad and make conflicts worse when they are sinful. Sin is doing what God forbids or refusing to do what God commands. (When we sin, we are more interested in pleasing ourselves than in obeying God.) We can learn what God commands and forbids by reading the Bible. Here are a few examples of sinful choices: throwing a temper tantrum, arguing, nagging, pouting, breaking any of the Ten Commandments, or being self-centered.

Teaching Tip

Use Worksheet One—Identifying Choices (Appendix C) as a visual aid to reinforce this concept. List some ideas of good and bad choices that students make. Use an overhead or the blackboard so that children can easily see the lists. Reinforce the fact that they will need to depend on God's help if they are going to make good choices consistently.

Choices are good and can lead to solutions to conflicts when they are: respectful, obedient, considerate, truthful, right according to Scripture, and God-centered.

- **What kind of choices did Tony make?** (Bad ones)

- **What were they?** (Tony chose to argue with his mother, stomp out of the room, and slam the door.)

- **What good choices could Tony have made instead?** (Tony could have listened to his mother and considered the report about the severe storm warning; expressed his disappointment, but accepted his mother's decision without arguing; expressed gratitude that his mother heard the weather report and cared about his safety; called Eric to explain why he was not able to go to the movie that day.)

Tony was in conflict with his mother because of his bad choices that came from his selfish heart.

The Bible says that children are to honor their father and mother (Exod. 20:12). Tony chose to disobey this commandment by speaking and acting disrespectfully toward his mother. Disobeying God's Word is always serious!

- **Did Tony's mother make him choose to argue or slam the door?** (No! No one made Tony respond as he did. Each person involved in a conflict makes his or her own choices as to how he or she will respond to the situation.)

- **Did Tony's mother contribute to this conflict in any way?** (Tony's mother spoke disrespectfully to Tony when she screamed at him. She needs to consider her example to Tony. Does she yell, argue and slam doors? Perhaps she also needs to ask the Lord to help her to change the ways she handles anger or conflict.)

Resisting Selfish Desires

Even though Tony had a strong, selfish desire to go to the movie that afternoon, he did not have to make sinful choices to argue with his mother, stomp away, and slam the door. He did not have to let his desires control him. We all act like Tony sometimes. We want our own way and we make selfish choices to get it.

- **What choices do you make to get what you want? What other choices could you make instead?**

Points to remember:

- Your choices are deliberate.
- Your choices are your responsibility.
- Your choices are your fault.
- You are one-hundred-percent responsible for your own choices!
- You will make good or bad choices depending on what is in your heart.

Role Play Activity: Choose a number of students to act out examples of good choices Tony could have made in this situation.

Good Reasons for Conflict

Many conflicts happen because you want your own way and make choices to get it. These are bad reasons for conflict. However, there are some good reasons to get into a conflict. The following are examples of good choices you could make that might lead to a conflict.

1. Obeying God by Standing Up for What You Believe Is Right

There may be times when someone will try to get you to do something that you know is wrong, such as stealing or telling a lie. You may be tempted to do the wrong thing out of fear of what your friends might think of you. Even though it may be hard to stand up for what is right, you need to tell others that what they're asking is wrong and you will not do it. At that point you will probably find yourself in a conflict with others, but it is a necessary or a good kind of conflict because you are standing up for what you know is right.

At times you may find yourself in a conflict because of your Christian beliefs. As Christians, we are called to stand up for Jesus and what he teaches in the Bible. This often causes conflict. This kind of conflict depends on doing what is right according to the Bible, instead of what is wrong and sinful. In these circumstances there is good reason for conflict. God's Word is always right, and ideas or actions that oppose God's Word are always wrong.

■ **In the story about Tony, who was standing up for what was right?** (Tony's mother)

■ **Why do you think so?** (Tony's mother knew that the weather conditions were dangerous that afternoon.

She needed to stand up for what was right by refusing to allow Tony to be out in a severe storm. Since Tony's mother is saying no to the movie because of the weather conditions, Tony needs to accept her decision without arguing.)

■ **How would Tony stand up for what is right?** (He would pray for a heart that is willing to be obedient. He would tell Eric that he is not allowed to go to the movie. Even if Eric gets upset, Tony needs to respectfully stand up for what is right. He could say, "I'm sorry that you are upset, Eric. I want to go, too, but I believe that I need to obey my mother. She doesn't want us to get hurt. Maybe we can go next Saturday instead.")

■ **Can you think of some examples of times you should stand up for doing right?** (Saying no to peer pressure when you know it's wrong—for instance, when kids urge you to drink or take drugs, not to do your work, ignore or hurt someone, steal, or lie.)

Good conflicts can turn into bad conflicts if you make sinful or selfish choices to make your point. You will need to use self-control to keep yourself from being rude, hurtful, or disrespectful. We will be talking more about this in later lessons. Now let's look at another good reason to get into a conflict.

2. Sharing Your Opinions with Others Who Think Differently than You Do

Some conflicts occur when people have different opinions. Differences of opinion are okay in matters of likes and dislikes (personal preferences). For instance, some people like baseball and some like basketball; some like piano and some like violin; some like ice cream and some like yogurt.

In your heart you may feel threatened or insecure when others don't agree with you or don't like what you like. You may feel as if your opinions are wrong instead of just different. Keep in mind that people will not always think alike or agree with each other. When you become angry with someone for not agreeing with you, or you say hurtful things to that person, then you have created bad conflict, which can hurt your relationship. This does not please God. On the other hand, if you talk about your opinions in a respectful way, you can be confident that God will be honored and you will be blessed, even though you may be in a conflict with someone.

Point to remember: Having a different opinion about personal preferences is not wrong. But making fun of a person for not having the same opinion or belief is wrong and sinful, and often causes conflict.

CONFLICT STARTS IN THE HEART.

Wrapping It Up

We know that **conflict starts in the heart.** You will have good desires as well as bad ones that take root in your heart. If you make choices to satisfy your selfish desires, then you shouldn't be surprised when you get into conflict. We also learned that choices are deliberate and there is a relationship between your heart, your choices, and your conflicts. We discussed the fact that there are good and bad conflicts, as well as respectful and disrespectful choices in those conflicts. Remember, good conflicts can become bad ones if you make disrespectful choices during the conflicts. When you give in to your selfish desires and choose to fight, argue, throw a temper tantrum, ridicule and criticize others while in a conflict, the conflict becomes bad and sinful.

Jesus is always ready to forgive you if you confess your sinful desires and choices (1 John 1:9). Jesus will also help you to make good choices even when you are in a conflict. Remember he is a faithful God who keeps his promises to help his children to become more like him. Let's decide today to depend on Jesus to help us make good choices.

Closing Prayer

Dear Lord, sometimes when I get into conflicts, I blame others for my choices instead of taking responsibility for what I choose to do and say. Please forgive me and help me to accept that my choices are my own. Show me what I can learn from conflict so that I can be more like you. Help me to understand what is at the root of my sinful choices, and give me a new heart and fill it with desires that please and honor you. In Jesus' name,
Amen.

Making It Real

Assign one or more of the suggested activities for Lesson Two that are found in the Activities and Personal Application section of this lesson. Some of the activities are included in Student Activity Book #2.

Activities and Personal Application

Activities one and two can be found in Student Activity Book (SAB) #2.

1. Root and Fruit Maze (see SAB 2-9): See if you can match up the "root" and the "fruit." Trace through the tangle of roots to find what is in the heart that causes each person to think, speak, or act the way they do.

2. Monster Scramble (see SAB 2-10): Draw arrows to connect the good desires to the monster desires, and the monster desires to the bad consequences. (Answers: 2-9-11...3-6-12... 4-10-13...5-7-15).

3. Complete Worksheet One— Identifying Choices (Appendix C). Think of good and bad choices that you make or have made in the past. List your choices in the proper categories.

4. Write a story about a conflict you read about in a book or saw on TV.

- Tell how the fight began.
- Identify the root cause of the conflict.
- Explain what choices each person made to cause the conflict.
- What lessons can each person learn from being in this conflict?
- What respectful choices could have prevented this conflict?
- Illustrate your story.
- Be prepared to read your story and show your picture in class.

5. Draw a picture or a cartoon strip of two people having a conflict.

6. With your parents, make a list of good things that God could be teaching you through conflict. Write a personal prayer about the conflict.

7. Have children work in small groups to develop a puppet play about conflict. If time allows, they can make their puppets. You may provide puppets or stuffed animals to save time.

8. Make a conflict collage. Cut and paste pictures from magazines that show people in conflict.

Dig into the Word

Memory Verse:

James 4:1-2

Other Relevant Bible Verses:

Proverbs 26:20
Matthew 5:3-12
Luke 6:43-45
1 Corinthians 12:12-31

Applicable Bible Stories:

Assign one or more of the following passages to help children analyze conflict situations in the Bible.

Cain's response to Abel (Gen. 4:1-8)

Abram and Lot (Gen. 13:1-12)

Jacob's response to his brother's claim to the birthright (Gen. 27:1-40)

Jacob's sons' response to Joseph when he became his father's favorite (Gen. 37:1-36)

The fiery furnace (Dan. 3:1-30)

Daniel and the lions' den (Dan. 6:1-28)

The Lesson Summary

Bible Memory Verse

"What causes fights and quarrels among you? Don't they come from your desires that battle within you? You want something but don't get it" (James 4:1-2).

Key Principle

Conflict starts in the heart.

The Main Points of This Lesson

1. Where does conflict come from?

Most conflicts happen because people make choices to get their own way. These choices usually come from selfish desires that are rooted in their hearts. Examples of root desires that lead to selfish choices:

Selfishness:	You want your own way.
Self-pity:	You feel sorry for yourself and you want others to feel sorry for you, too.
Greed:	You want more and you are not content with what you have.
Pride:	You think you are better than others.
Fear of others.	You are afraid of what others think of you. You want to be liked.

You do not need to be controlled by these selfish desires. If you ask God, he will begin to replace them with the desire to love and please him, which will lead to good choices.

2. What causes conflict?

People make deliberate choices to satisfy their desires. In other words, they make choices on purpose.
Everyone is one hundred percent responsible for their own choices.
Two categories of choices that people make are:

● Good	● Bad
● Right	● Wrong
● Obedient	● Disobedient
● Respectful	● Disrespectful
● Wise	● Foolish
● Righteous	● Sinful

3. Good reasons for conflict

You need to obey God by standing up for something you believe is right. It's okay to share different opinions. However, it is wrong to put others down if they don't share the same opinion.

Choices Have Consequences

Do not
deceive
yourselves;
no one
makes a
fool of God.
A man will
reap
exactly what
he
plants.

Galations 6:7
(Today's English Version).

Lesson Goal:

To help children understand the relationship between choices and consequences.

Lesson Objectives:

By God's grace children will learn:
1. That choices have consequences.
2. That just as their choices belong to them, so do their consequences.

Key Principle:

Choices have consequences.

Lesson Needs:

Bible
Student Activity Book #3
Worksheet Two—Choices Have
  Consequences (Appendix C)

Begin with Prayer

Open with prayer that your students will understand that **choices have consequences** and that their consequences are directly related to the choices they make. Pray that they will be willing to take responsibility for both their choices and their consequences.

Review and Setting the Stage

We recently began to talk about conflict and how it affects you.

- **What is conflict?** (A fight between people who think or act differently.)

- **What are some synonyms for conflict?** (Fight/quarrel/disagreement/argument.)

- **How do people often respond to conflict?** (Briefly review the slippery slope.)

- **What is often at the root of choices that cause conflict?** (Sinful desires that control the heart.)

- **Name examples of good and bad choices.** (Right/wrong, obedient/disobedient, respectful/disrespectful, wise/foolish, righteous/sinful.)

- **Did anyone make choices that caused a conflict since last week? Briefly describe what you did.** (Accept short, appropriate descriptions of conflict situations.)

Today we are going to discuss the relationship between choices and consequences.

- **Does anyone know what a consequence is?** (Synonyms: result, effect, outcome.)

- **When do people usually get a consequence?** (After they have made a choice.)

- **Can you think of some possible consequences for the following choices?**

  - Jump off a high fence — sprain or break your ankle.

  - Touch a hot burner—get burned.

  - Do your schoolwork neatly and accurately—get good grades.

  - Speak respectfully to others— people will usually listen to you and respond respectfully.

Consequences Are Not New

ADAM & EVE

Consequences are not new. Adam and Eve were the first people to receive consequences from God. God told Adam that he was not to eat the fruit from a certain tree in the Garden. God also told Adam that if he did eat the fruit of that certain tree, he would die. God taught Adam to make good choices and warned him of the consequences of disobedience.

"The Lord God took the man and put him in the Garden of Eden to work it and take care of it. And the Lord God commanded the man, 'You are free to eat from any tree in the garden; but you must not eat from the tree of the knowledge of good and evil, for when you eat of it you will surely die'" (Gen. 2:15-17).

Adam and Eve disobeyed God. Both of them ate the fruit from the tree that God said was off limits to them. Their bodies did not die right then, but their perfect relationship with God was affected. When they made the choice to disobey God, they sinned, and they received a consequence for their sin. From that time on God promised that when anyone chooses to sin by disobeying what God's Word says there will be consequences. In the New Testament God says: "Do not deceive yourselves; no one makes a fool of God. A man will reap exactly what he plants" (Gal. 6:7, TEV).

This Bible verse teaches us that everyone gets consequences for choices, because God set it up that way.

CHOICES HAVE CONSEQUENCES.

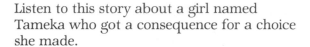

Tardy for the Party
featuring
TAMEKA & JENNY

Listen to this story about a girl named Tameka who got a consequence for a choice she made.

Tameka and her sister, Jenny, knew they were supposed to be home from playing at Sarah's house by 5:30 in the afternoon. Their family needed to be at the baseball field by six o'clock. Their brother, Chadwick, was playing in the city championship game, and the whole family planned to be there to cheer for his team. That morning Mom and Dad announced that they were going to take the family out for pizza as a special treat after the game. Before Tameka and Jenny went to Sarah's house, their mother reminded them to be home on time because of the fun night ahead. The girls were having so much fun at Sarah's house, that when Jenny reminded Tameka that it was time to go, Tameka said, "I'm going to stay here just a little longer. Besides, Mom and Dad will wait until I get home to go to the game." Jenny took off without Tameka so she would be home on time. Finally, at six o'clock Tameka decided that she needed to go home. When she walked in the front door, the house was unusually quiet. Tameka found a note from her parents:

Dear Tameka,

We have gone to Chadwick's game and then we are going out for pizza. I called Sarah's mother and she said you were still playing in their back yard. Since you knew what time to be home, and you chose not to be here, we left without you. We made arrangements for Jody Larson to stay with you for the evening. She will be here a little after six o'clock. We told her not to allow any TV, videos, or computer games tonight. We are feeling sad that you won't be with us tonight, but as you know, in our family **choices have consequences.**

Love,
Mom and Dad

Tameka received a consequence for her choice to come home late. She may feel that her parents are being unfair or even unloving, but actually they are demonstrating their love for her and helping her to learn how to make better choices in the future. Let's look at some important facts about choices and consequences.

Choose Your Consequences

When you make a choice, you also choose the consequences that go with it. The consequence dial shows how this works.

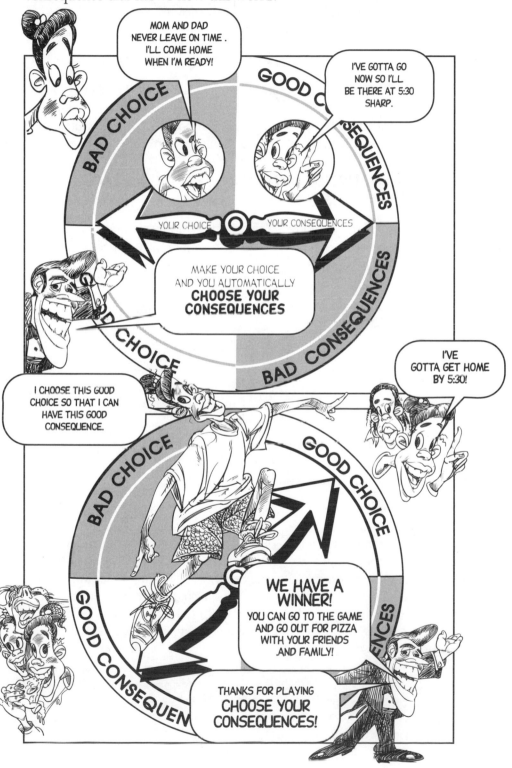

Choices Have Consequences

- **What do you get if you plant a rose bush?** (That's right! You get roses!)
- **What do you get if you plant weeds?** (That's right! You get weeds!)
- **What will happen if you make a good or bad choice?**
  (Right! You will get a good or bad consequence.)

Consequences Come after Choices

You will usually get consequences for your choices. Consequences can be immediate or delayed; they can be *natural* (like a broken leg from jumping from a tree) or *imposed* *on you* (like discipline for deliberate disobedience). Whether immediate or delayed, natural or imposed, your consequences depend on your choices.

There Are Consequences for Good and Bad Choices

Teaching Tip

Use Worksheet 2—**Choices Have Consequences** (Appendix C) as a visual aid to reinforce this concept. List examples of good and bad choices and their corresponding or predictable consequences to help the children understand the relationship between choices and consequences. I suggest that an overhead or blackboard be used in a classroom so that children can easily see the lists.

It's important to realize that not all consequences are bad. When you make a good choice any of the following consequences could be yours:

- Praise
- Thanks/appreciation
- Rewards
- Privileges
- Trust
- Confidence
- Clear Conscience

On the other hand, whenever you make a bad choice, you can expect the following consequences:

- Discipline or punishment
- No Rewards
- Lose Privileges
- Lose Trust
- No confidence
- Guilty conscience
- Restitution*

*■ **Does anyone know what restitution means?** (Restitution is making right what you did wrong. For example, you might have to pay for or replace something that you damaged, or clean up a mess you made. See Luke 19:8.)

Tameka and Jenny are learning that **choices have consequences**. Jenny earned the privilege to go to the game and then out for pizza with the family by coming home on time, while Tameka lost the same privilege due to her choice to stay longer at Sarah's house. The girls deserved different consequences because they made different choices. Tameka chose to stay longer than she was supposed to, therefore it was her own fault that she lost the privilege to join her family for the fun evening they had planned. Even if Sarah had pleaded with the girls to stay, it was Tameka's choice to do so. Jenny made the more responsible choice to go home on time, and consequently enjoyed being with her family for the game and for pizza.

Role Play Activity: Pretend to be Tameka, Jenny, their parents, and Sarah. In this role play act out a different ending to this story, where Tameka receives good consequences for her choice.

- Can you remember a time when you earned a good consequence for a choice you made? How did you feel?

- Can you remember a bad consequence you received for a choice you made? How did you feel?

- Which consequences did you like best: the good consequences or the bad consequences? Why?

Let's look at two choices and try to predict their consequences.

Choice:
- Finish your schoolwork

Predictable Consequences:
- Better grades or other rewards
- Go out for recess and go home on time
- Earn a good reputation with others
- Sense of personal accomplishment
- Parents and teachers are pleased
- Develop diligence and perseverance

- **What is the only way to get these good consequences?** (To make the choice to complete your schoolwork and to do a good job.)

Choice:
- Don't finish your schoolwork

Predictable Consequences:
- Lower grades and no rewards
- Stay in for recess or stay after school to do the work
- Earn a bad reputation with others
- Parents and teachers don't trust you to make good choices
- Fear of getting caught

- **How can you prevent bad consequences?** (By making the good choice to complete your work and do a good job.)

Role Play Activity: Without asking for permission, Kari borrowed her sister's new sweater to wear to her friend's birthday party. While at the party Kari spilled a glass of raspberry punch down the front of the sweater. Act out what Kari should do about this situation. Make sure to include in your role play the types of consequences that would be appropriate.

- **How could Kari have prevented her bad consequences?** (By asking for permission before she used the sweater; by trying to be more careful so as not to spill food or drinks on her clothes.)

Consequences Belong to You

After people make choices, they will often try to avoid the consequences by blaming someone else or lying about what they did. (We'll talk about this more in a later chapter.) It is important to understand that *the person who makes a choice deserves the consequence.* For instance, if you make a choice, it is not your parent's fault if you receive a consequence. Remember that consequences are directly related to your choices. As Tameka's parents might say to her:

"You made the choice to come home late. Now your consequence is that you will not get to go out for pizza with us."

Arguing About Your Consequences

Sometimes you will be tempted to argue and quarrel with the person who is giving you the consequence you deserve. However, before you do that, remember that you made a choice and now you are receiving your consequence. Just as your choices belong to you, so do your consequences. God wants you to respectfully accept the consequences for your choices without arguing or quarreling.

Avoiding Your Consequences

You may also be tempted to use excuses to get out of your consequences. A typical excuse is, "I forgot." Sometimes you will forget things, but you should never use "I forgot" as an excuse to avoid deserved consequences. Hopefully, you will learn to be more careful to remember in the future.

Consequences are necessary to help you to remember to change bad choices to good ones. God loves you too much to let you do whatever you want, and he promises that his children will have consequences for disobeying his Word. The consequences may be immediate or they may be delayed, but they will occur. Remember that the Apostle Paul said: "Do not deceive yourselves; no one makes a fool of God. A man will reap exactly what he plants" (Gal. 6:7, TEV).

God has given certain people the authority and the responsibility to give consequences when necessary.

■ **Do you know to whom the Lord gives authority to give consequences to his people?**

● Parents have authority in the *family* (see Eph. 6:1-3).

● Church leaders have authority in the *church* (see Titus 3:1-2).

● Police, school officials, or lawmakers have authority in the *government* (see Rom. 13:1-7).

You may try to get out of consequences because you fear what they will be. The Bible says *that people usually do not have to fear consequences if they do what is right.* Many people fear getting caught for making bad (sinful) choices, because they don't want to receive the consequences. Listen to what the Apostle Paul says in Romans 13:3: "Do you want to be free from fear of the one in authority? Then do what is right and he will commend you."

Changing Your Consequences

When you are receiving a bad consequence (like discipline or punishment) from a person in authority, you will probably not feel happy about it. You may even feel that the person does not love or understand you. Always remember that your choices belong to you. *If you don't like your consequences, you can change your choices.*

"My son, do not make light of the Lord's discipline, and do not lose heart when he rebukes you, because the Lord disciplines those he loves, and he punishes everyone he accepts as a son. God disciplines us for our good, that we may share in his holiness" (Heb. 12:6, 10).

The purpose of loving discipline is to help you to grow in holiness and self-discipline. You must understand that the person who properly disciplines you really loves you.

Preventing Bad Consequences

The best way to prevent conflict and avoid bad consequences is to depend on God to help you to:

- Make good choices (Gal. 6:9).
- Do what is right (Mic. 6:8).
- Obey people in authority—as long as they don't tell you to do something wrong (Eph. 6:1-3).
- Speak and act respectfully to all people (Eph. 4:29).

Then you will not have to fear authority or consequences (Rom. 13:3). Instead you will enjoy good consequences and a clear conscience (Acts 24:16).

Sometimes it is hard to make right choices, isn't it? The good news is that Jesus will help you. He doesn't expect you to do what is right all by yourself. The Apostle Paul reminds us that: "I can do everything through him who gives me strength" (Phil. 4:13).

YOU CHOOSE
YOUR CONSEQUENCES
BY THE CHOICES
YOU MAKE.

Wrapping It Up

In this lesson we learned that **choices have consequences**, and that the person who makes a choice deserves the consequences. When we make good choices, it is likely that we will receive good consequences. However, if we choose to sin by making bad choices, then we shouldn't be surprised or angry if we receive bad consequences. We are only getting what we deserve. We may try to fool people to avoid our consequences, but we can never deceive God. He promises that we will "reap exactly what we plant," either good or bad. Always remember that the Holy Spirit will give you the power you need to make good choices.

Closing Prayer

Dear Lord, thank you for loving me as I am. I know that there are many times when I sin, not only by doing wrong, but also when I don't do what is right. I even try to avoid the consequences by lying or blaming someone else for my choices. Please forgive me, Lord. Help me to be more honest about the choices I make and more accepting of the consequences I deserve. In Jesus' name,
Amen.

Making It Real

Assign one or more of the suggested activities for Lesson Three that are found in the Activities and Personal Application section of this lesson. Some of the activities are included in Student Activity Book #3.

Activities and Personal Application

Activities one, two, three, and four can be found in Student Activity Book (SAB) #3.

1. Crossword review (see SAB 3-8): Review the concepts we have learned by completing the crossword puzzle. (Answers: 1-Heart 2-Good desires 3-Deliberately 4-Choices 5-Consequences 6-Selfish)

2. Dear Constance Quence (see SAB 3-8): Practice giving good advice by answering each of the questions about choices and consequences.

3. It's Nothing New—We Get What's Due (see SAB 3-9): Read the Bible stories, then identify the choice that each person made and the consequences that resulted from the choice.

4. Pay the Price, Now or Later (see SAB 3-10): Imagine that you break a neighbor's window with your frisbee. Decide what consequences will flow from different choices.

5. Tell about a time when you made a good or a bad choice. What were your consequences for your choice? Explain how you handled your consequences. Do you think you will continue to make that same choice? Why or why not?

6. Using Worksheet Two—Choices Have Consequences (Appendix C), write down an example of a good choice and the opposite bad choice. Then list some predictable consequences for each choice. The more personal the choices, the more meaningful the assignment will be.

7. Read the following Bible passages and record the consequences that the Israelites were told they could expect for their choices.
- Deuteronomy 11:13-15
- Deuteronomy 11:16-17
- 2 Chronicles 7:14
- Jeremiah 17:24-26
- Jeremiah 17:27

Dig into the Word

Memory Verse:

Galatians 6:7

Other Relevant Bible Verses:

1 Corinthians 15:33
Galatians 6:7-10
Ephesians 5:5-7
Hebrews 12:7-11

Applicable Bible Stories:

Assign one or more of the following passages to help children analyze conflict situations in the Bible.

Joseph refuses to be immoral (Gen. 39:1-20; but see also 39:21-23 and 41:1-44)

Aaron's response to the Israelites' demands for a golden calf (Ex. 32:1-6)

Moses' response to the Israelites who worshiped the golden calf (Ex. 32:18-35)

Miriam and Aaron oppose Moses (Num. 12:1-15)

Shadrach, Meshach, and Abednego refuse to worship the image of gold (Dan. 3:1-30).

The Lesson Summary

Bible Memory Verse

"Do not deceive yourselves; no one makes a fool of God. A man will reap exactly what he plants" (Gal. 6:7, TEV).

Key Principle

Choices have consequences.

The Main Points of This Lesson

1. Choices have consequences
Consequences come after choices.
There are consequences for good and bad choices.
Good consequences include:

- Praise
- Thanks and appreciation
- Privileges
- Rewards
- Trust
- Confidence
- Clear conscience

Bad consequences include:

- Discipline/punishment
- Lose privileges
- Make restitution
- No rewards
- Lose trust
- No confidence
- Guilty conscience

(Restitution means that you pay for damages you have caused.)

2. Consequences belong to you.
The person who makes a choice deserves the consequence for that choice.
Just as your choices belong to you, so do your consequences. In other words, you are responsible for your own choices.
Consequences are necessary to help you remember to change bad choices to good ones.

Prevent bad consequences by asking God to help you:

- Make good choices.
- Do what is right.
- Obey people in authority (as long as they don't tell you to do something you know is wrong).
- Speak and act respectfully to all people.

Making Choices the Wise Way

The
wisdom
of the
prudent
is
to
**give
thought**
to their
ways.

Proverbs 14:8

Lesson Goal:

To help children discover the importance of thinking about their choices before making them.

Lesson Objectives:

By God's grace children will learn:
1. Two basic approaches to making choices.
2. That it is wise to seek godly advice.
3. That making wise choices can prevent conflict.

Key Principle:

Wise-way choices are better than my-way choices.

Lesson Needs:

Bible
Student Activity Book #4.

Begin with Prayer

Begin the lesson with an opening prayer that your students will understand the importance of making wise choices that prevent conflict instead of foolish choices that cause conflict.

Review and Setting the Stage

In lesson one, we talked about the slippery slope.

- **Do you remember what it is?** (An arc that describes the three types of responses to conflict.)

- **Do you remember what the three types of responses are?** (Escape, attack, work-it-out.)

- **How do people escape?** (Deny, blame game, run away.)

- **How do people attack?** (Put downs, gossip, fight.)

- **How do people work-it-out?** (Overlook the offense, talk, get help.)

We discovered that how we respond to conflict is a personal choice, and those choices will have consequences. When we choose to slide down the slippery slope into the attack or escape zones, we will often find ourselves in trouble with someone. However, when we choose to stay on top of the slippery slope and handle our fights and quarrels in a way that pleases God, we will usually find our conflicts resolved and our relationships secure.

- **Who is responsible for choices and consequences?** (The person who made the choice is responsible for that choice and for the resulting consequences.)

Oh No, Forgot to Mow!
featuring
CARLOS & MATT

In this lesson we are going to learn how to make wise choices that please God, keep us on top of the slippery slope, and usually result in good consequences. Wisdom is knowing and doing what God's Word says to do. Wise choices allow you to have a clear conscience and feel confident about your decisions. They also help to prevent conflict. Wise choices come from a humble heart that trusts and follows God's ways instead of doing what is selfish. Listen to a story about a boy who has to decide what kind of choice to make.

Carlos was up bright and early Saturday morning. He and his friend, Matt Johnson, had spent the whole week planning to go to the neighborhood gym to play basketball, and Carlos couldn't wait to get started. He was almost ready to go. All he had left to do was to wash the dishes, find his basketball, and wait for Matt and Mr. Johnson to pick him up. Just after Matt walked in, Carlos noticed a note from his father reminding him to mow the lawn before going to the gym. Carlos hadn't mowed the lawn on Friday as he said he would, and his dad remembered! He didn't feel like mowing the lawn now. He wanted to go to the gym to play basketball with Matt. He had looked forward to this game all week, and he wasn't going to let that dumb lawn get in the way of his fun.

Carlos has a choice to make. He can decide to do what he feels like doing, which will probably lead to trouble, or he can decide to do what he knows is right, which will please God and prevent a conflict with his father.

- **Have you ever had to choose between your selfish feelings and what you knew was the right thing to do?**

- **What were the consequences of your choice?**

- **How did you feel about making that choice? Would you make the same choice again?**

My-Way Choices and Wise-Way Choices

Look at what happens when we get into the habit of making my-way choices. We go around in circles without finding a way out of the problem.

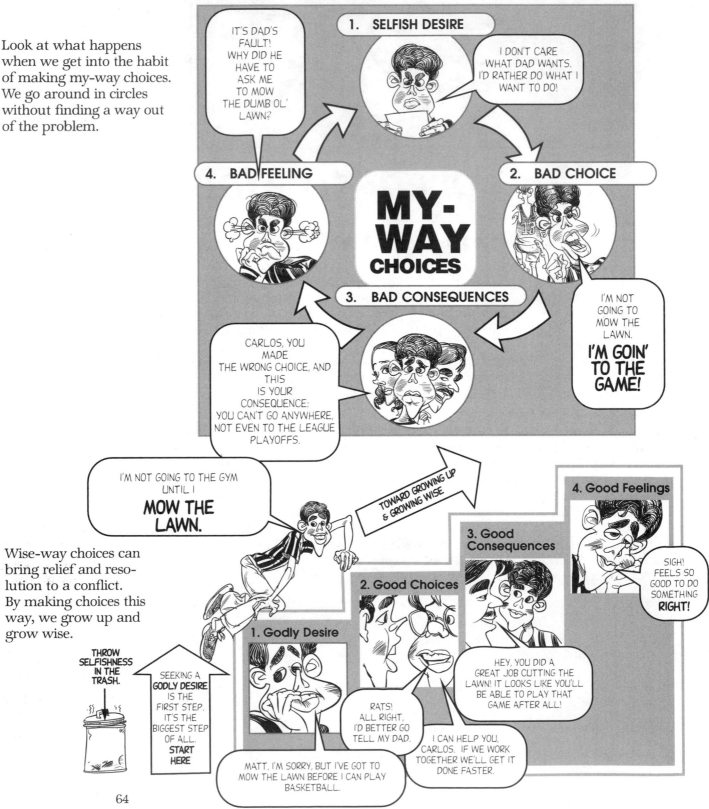

Wise-way choices can bring relief and resolution to a conflict. By making choices this way, we grow up and grow wise.

Making Choices

Let's explore two ways to make choices. One usually leads to trouble, while the other helps to solve problems.

- The "my-way" approach (Make choices that will only please and satisfy myself.)
- The "wise-way" approach (Make choices that will please and honor the Lord.)

The "My-way" Approach

The my-way approach goes like this: Something happens that triggers thoughts and desires inside of you. In response to this situation —

You have a SINFUL (SELFISH) DESIRE

that leads to a BAD CHOICE

and results in a BAD CONSEQUENCE

and BAD FEELINGS.

Let's consider Carlos' situation for a moment. Carlos' desire is to play basketball with his friend and not to mow the lawn this morning. If he uses the my-way approach, he will make choices that will satisfy his desires instead of choosing to do what would please God. Consequently, he could find himself in a conflict. Let's look at how this might work.

Desire: "I want to play basketball with Matt this morning! Why did Dad have to remind me that I have to mow the dumb lawn anyway? I don't want to do it today! I hate that job! I wish I never had to do it!"

Choice: "It's too late to mow the lawn today anyway. I'll just pretend I didn't see the note. Maybe I'll get to it later."

Consequences: Carlos will probably be disciplined when he gets home from the game. He will still have to mow the lawn. He may lose the privilege of going to the gym for a couple weeks. His parents will lose confidence and trust in him. They might put more limits on his time. He probably won't enjoy the game because of his guilty conscience.

Feelings: Carlos will feel angry, frustrated, and disappointed because of his conse-quences. He may also feel guilty, and while he is playing basketball he will be constantly thinking of excuses for not mowing the lawn. Because he fears his dad's response to this disobedience, he will not enjoy the game with Matt and his friends.

If Carlos develops the habit of using the my-way approach, he will probably reap bad consequences and feelings as a steady diet. All of us have felt like Carlos at times.

■ **Can you remember a time when someone upset your plans, hurt you, or didn't let you have your own way?**

(You probably struggled with selfish desires, and it's likely that you felt like getting back at the person. Let's say that your friend gets angry at you because you don't want to play the same game that she does. She calls you a name and even hits you. What do you feel like doing? My guess is that you will want to make a my-way choice and run away from the situation, or you will call her a name or even hit her. As we already learned, these escape and attack responses do not please the Lord, and they usually make conflicts worse. Consequently, my-way choices are foolish choices.)

■ **What will probably happen to your friendship if you make these choices?**
(You and your friend won't talk for a while; you could get into a fight; you'll be angry with each other; you could both get hurt; you might lose your friendship; you might get into trouble for fighting.)

WISE-WAY CHOICES ARE BETTER THAN MY-WAY CHOICES.

The "Wise-way" Approach

Now let's look at the other way to make choices. The wise-way approach is the smart way to make choices. It is the opposite of the my-way approach. Instead of giving in to your feelings and selfish desires, you can ask Jesus to help you make choices that will please him and prevent conflict.

When you choose the wise-way approach, you will first confess your sinful desires and feelings to the Lord and ask him for help so that your desire and your choice will please him. Your response will be more like this:

You confess your sinful desire

and pray for a DESIRE TO PLEASE GOD,

which leads to a GOOD CHOICE

and results in a GOOD CONSEQUENCE

and GOOD FEELINGS.

God empowers his children to use this approach when making choices, because it leads to wise choices more often. If Carlos would use this approach, something like this might happen.

Sinful Desire: *"Lord Jesus, please forgive me for being so selfish. I always want my own way and it only gets me into trouble. Please give me a willing heart to do what is right."*

Godly Desire: "Dad reminded me to mow the lawn before I go to the gym to play basketball today. It is my own fault that I did not mow it yesterday. I sure don't want to mow it today. But I know that I'll please the Lord and Dad if I obey now, so that makes it worthwhile."

Choice: I need to accept responsibility for the choice I made not to mow the lawn yesterday. I am just going to have to do it now. I know that this will disappoint Matt, and I will need to ask his forgiveness for ruining our plans. I just won't be able to play basketball this morning unless Matt will be willing to leave a little later.

Consequences: Carlos may be praised and thanked for doing a good job. He won't have to mow the lawn later. He will still get to play basketball if Matt is willing to leave later. He would have confidence in his decision. He would have a clear conscience knowing he did what he was supposed to do. His parents would have more confidence in Carlos and would trust him to be dependable. His parents may reward him in unexpected ways.

Feelings: Although Carlos will probably feel upset with himself for not mowing the lawn when he should have, he will feel confident that he made the right choice to get the job done before he went to the gym with Matt. If Matt is willing to leave later, Carlos will feel excited about getting to play basketball, and he will be glad that he has a clear conscience. He will feel proud that he pleased his father by doing such a good job on the lawn. He will feel relieved that he made a choice that he knew would please the Lord instead of himself.

Like Carlos, if you use the wise-way approach, you can experience the freedom, trust, confidence, and clear conscience that comes when you make good choices.

Remember, when you do only what satisfies your desires, you are using the my-way approach to making choices. This applies to choices you make to get your own way or to get back at someone who has upset you. If you get into the habit of making these kinds of choices, you may often find yourself in conflict with others, and you can expect bad consequences.

On the other hand, wise choices come from a humble heart that trusts God and desires to do what is right according to Scripture instead of what you feel like doing. The wise-way approach will please and honor God, keep you out of trouble, and help to solve problems. Clearly, **wise-way choices are better than my-way choices!**

Seeking Advice

God's Word explains the difference between someone who is foolish and does only what seems right to him, and one who is smart and gives thought to his choices. "The wisdom of the prudent is to give thought to their ways, but the folly of fools is deception" (Prov. 14:8).

Sometimes you might try to fool yourself by thinking that it would be best to do only what you feel like doing. Before you make the choice to follow your feelings, *you should ask someone you trust for advice.* You could ask your parents, a friend or relative, your teacher, or your pastor to help you do what is right. Then be smart and listen to their advice. "He who walks with the wise grows wise, but a companion of fools suffers harm" (Prov. 13:20).

Often you may be tempted to get advice from people who will say what you want to hear. They will tell you to do whatever you want to do. That kind of advice is dangerous and foolish when it comes to deciding what is right and wrong. It is important to be careful to get advice that will help you to please and glorify God! "The way of the fool seems right to him, but a wise man listens to advice" (Prov. 12:15).

Preventing Conflict

Hopefully, by now you can see that **wise-way choices are better than my-way choices,** and they can help prevent conflict. Let's practice making wise-way choices.

Seek Godly Advice

"Plans fail for lack of counsel, but with many advisers they succeed" (Prov. 15:22).

> **Role Play Activity:** You are in a conflict with your sister about the closet space you share. Her things are always piled up on your side of the closet, resulting in many conflicts. You decide to get advice from your mother on how to handle this problem.

Make Right Choices

"Let us not become weary in doing good, for at the proper time we will reap a harvest if we do not give up" (Gal. 6:9).

> **Role Play Activity:** Your friend stops by your house to ask you to go to the park. Your mother told you to clean up the family room while she is at the store because the new neighbors are coming over this evening. This is the third time this week that you would miss doing something fun with your friend. Act out two responses to your friend's request. Make sure one of them is a right choice.

Do What Is Right According to the Bible

"Your word is a lamp to my feet and a light for my path" (Ps. 119:105).

"He has showed you, O man, what is good. And what does the Lord require of you? To act justly and to love mercy and to walk humbly with your God" (Mic. 6:8).

> **Role Play Activity:** Your brother asked you to forgive him for getting mad and yelling at you during the swim team tryouts. He knew that it was wrong to embarrass you. First act out what you would feel like saying to him. Now act out the right way to respond to him according to the Bible.

Obey Your Parents and Others in Authority

"Children, obey your parents in the Lord, for this is right. 'Honor your father and mother'— which is the first commandment with a promise—'that it may go well with you and that you may enjoy long life on the earth'" (Eph. 6:1-2).

> **Role Play Activity:** Your cousin's friend asks you if you want to listen to her new CD. It's recorded by a group that your parents do not allow you to listen to. The girl makes fun of you when you tell her that you are not allowed to listen to that group. Act out the wrong and right ways to respond to her.

Speak and Act Respectfully to Everyone

"Do not let any unwholesome talk come out of your mouths, but only what is helpful for building others up according to their needs, that it may benefit those who listen" (Eph. 4:29).

> **Role Play Activity:** You are on a Little League baseball team. During a play-off game your coach yells at you because you missed catching a fly ball. Act out how you can respectfully respond to your coach.

Teaching Tip

Re-explain to your children that they need to obey only what is consistent with God's Word. They never need to obey a person if they are told to sin. If they are unsure whether to obey or not, they should seek advice from someone trustworthy.

Wrapping It Up

In this lesson we learned that there are two ways to make choices: The wise-way approach, which is the smart way, or the my-way approach, which is foolish and usually gets us into trouble. When we use the wise-way to make our choices, we can feel confident that we have been wise, we have pleased the Lord, and we will usually prevent conflict and stay out of trouble.

When we face difficult choices, it is wise to seek advice from someone who can help us make a wise decision that is consistent with God's Word. Keep in mind what Proverbs 12:15 says: "The way of the fool seems right to him, but a wise man listens to advice." Remember that **wise-way choices are better than my-way choices.** Let's ask God for help right now.

Closing Prayer

Dear Lord, thank you for being my wise Father and Friend. So often I make foolish choices. Please forgive me. Help me to look at my choices honestly and to think of ways to change those foolish choices that make you sad and get me into conflict with others. Please show me how to be wise so that I can learn to please you with my choices. Help me to take responsibility for preventing conflict by making choices the wise way. In Jesus' name,

Amen.

Making It Real

Assign one or more of the suggested activities for Lesson Four that are found in the Activities and Personal Application section of this lesson. Some of the activities are included in Student Activity Book #4.

Activities and Personal Application

Activities one, two, and three can be found in Student Activity Book (SAB) #4.

1. The Prodigal's My-way and Wise-way Choices (see SAB 4-8): Read the story about the prodigal son and decide what part of the my-way sequence and the wise-way sequence describes his thoughts, words, and actions.

2. Slip, Slop, or Stay on Top (see SAB 4-9): Draw a line from each of the choices to the matching response on the slippery slope. Then go back and cross out all of the my-way choices and circle all of the wise-way choices.

3. Oops I Blew It (see SAB 4-10): Using the my-way diagram, describe a time when you made a my-way choice.

4. You are John's friend. One day he comes to you for advice about Clay. Clay is a new boy who has just moved into John's neighborhood and is pressuring him to sneak out Friday night for a party. John's parents are concerned about Clay's negative influence on their son. When they discuss their concerns with John, he agrees that there is a foundation for their fears. But John still likes Clay. He wants to be his friend, but he doesn't want to get into trouble. John asks you what he should do.

Explain your advice in a way that helps John identify the consequences of both his good and his bad choices in this situation.

5. Poster Contest: Design a conflict poster that shows how to keep out of conflict. (This can be done individually or as a class.) BE CREATIVE!

6. Make up a story or draw a cartoon strip about a person who made a my-way choice rather than a wise-way choice. Tell what consequences followed the choice, and how the person felt about his or her choice. Include in your story what the person could have done differently. You can act out your story for your family or class.

Dig into the Word

Memory Verse:

Proverbs 14:8

Other Relevant Bible Verses:

Foolish Choices:
Psalm 14:1
Proverbs 10:14
Proverbs 12:15-16
Proverbs 13:20
Proverbs 14:16
Proverbs 15:5
Proverbs 18:2
Proverbs 20:3
Proverbs 28:26

Wise choices:
Proverbs 3:5-6
Proverbs 3:13
Proverbs 13:10
Proverbs 16:23
Proverbs 29:25
Additional Verses:
Micah 6:8
Galatians 6:9
Ephesians 4:29
Ephesians 6:1-2

Applicable Bible Stories:

Assign one or more of the following passages to help children analyze conflict situations in the Bible.

Daniel's response to the command to eat unclean food (Dan. 1:8-16)

Jonah learns to obey God (Jonah 1:1-3:3)

The prodigal son and his forgiving father (Luke 15:11-24)

The Apostles' response to the demand that they stop preaching the gospel (Acts 5:27-42)

The Lesson Summary

Bible Memory Verse

"The wisdom of the prudent is to give thought to their ways" (Prov. 14:8).

Key Principle

Wise-way choices are better than my-way choices.

The Main Points of This Lesson

1. Two ways to make choices

- The my-way approach
- The wise-way approach

The my-way approach goes like this:

- You have a sinful desire
- that leads to a bad choice
- and results in a bad consequence
- and bad feelings.

The wise-way approach goes like this:

- You confess your sinful desire
- and pray for a desire to please God,
- which leads to a good choice
- and results in a good consequence
- and good feelings.

2. Seek godly advice

If you are not sure about what choice to make, you should ask someone you trust for advice. You could ask your parents, a friend or relative, your teacher, or your pastor to help you decide what is right.

You may be tempted to get advice from people who will say what you want to hear. They will tell you to do whatever you want to do. That kind of advice is dangerous and foolish when it comes to deciding what is right and wrong.

3. Wise choices can prevent conflict

Foolish choices come from a proud, self-centered heart that is only concerned about satisfying selfish desires. Foolish choices often cause conflict.

Wise choices come from a humble heart that trusts God and wants to do what is right according to the Bible. Wise choices usually prevent conflict.

Part Two
Responding to Conflict

Confession is not a popular concept in today's society. We are quick to blame others for our problems and our choices. Frequently we claim, "It's not my fault," even when it is! This attitude is not unique to this decade. Adam and Eve were the first people to deny responsibility for their choices, and people have practiced the art of blaming ever since. Since taking responsibility is not consistently modeled even in the church, these next four lessons are crucial if children are going to have a godly attitude toward conflict and learn to respond to it biblically.

In this section you will teach children to recognize their tendency to blame others for their choices. Next, they will see that conflict is an opportunity to glorify God, serve other people, and grow in Christ-likeness. They will also learn to respond to conflict in a reasonable, responsible, and biblical manner. Finally, they will learn how to confess their wrongs and forgive others as God has forgiven them.

Playing the Blame Game

> ## He who conceals his sins does not prosper, but whoever confesses and renounces them finds mercy.
>
> Proverbs 28:13

Lesson Goal:

To help children understand their tendency to blame others for conflict.

Lesson Objectives:

By God's grace children will learn:
1. What it means to play the blame game.
2. That playing the blame game can cause double trouble.
3. That playing the blame game gives them an excuse to feel like a victim.
4. That there is help to resist the blame game and change choices.

Key Principle:

The blame game makes conflict worse.

Lesson Needs:

Bible
Student Activity Book #5

Begin with Prayer

Begin with a prayer that reflects the objectives of the lesson. Pray that your students will understand what the blame game is and resolve not to play it. Pray that they will put themselves at the mercy of Christ, not other people.

Review and Setting the Stage

- **What is the difference between wise-way and my-way choices?** (Wise-way choices glorify God, are obedient to God's Word, and come from a desire to please God. My-way choices satisfy selfish, sinful desires and often lead to conflict.)

- **Which of the slippery slope responses are wise?** (The work-it-out responses.)

- **Why are wise-way choices better than my-way choices?** (Accept appropriate answers.)

This week we are going to talk about playing a game. Not just any game, but the blame game. This is a game that we have all played at one time or another.

- **What do you think I mean when I say "playing the blame game?"** (When we refuse to take responsibility for our part in a conflict.)

Teaching Tip

If time permits, discuss one or more of the assigned activities from the previous lesson as a review. Collect and evaluate any assignments that are not discussed in class, and return them to the students with your comments so they can see that doing their homework is worthwhile.

Bully Bumps and Blames

featuring
NIKKI & SAMMIE

We often play the blame game after making a bad choice, because we want to avoid the consequences for our choices. Listen to a story about two children who are tempted to play the blame game because of choices they made.

It was a scorcher with temperatures soaring way above normal. Mr. Chung's students had just finished a spirited game of soccer and were on their way back to class. Most of them stopped at the water fountain for a cool drink before hurrying on to their room. Nikki was standing in line waiting her turn when "Sammie," short for Samantha, barged in front of her saying, "Out of my way, Nich-o-las!"

"No way, Sam-u-el! I was here first!" retorted Nikki, who was tired of the way Sammie tried to bully her and everyone else in her class. This time Nikki wasn't going to give in to Sammie's demands.

"Samuel? I'm no boy! Now get out of my way, Ol' St. Nich-o-las! I'm thirsty," snarled Sammie. With that, Nikki pushed Sammie out of line, yelling, "I'm not giving cuts!" Sammie fell against the wall and broke her glasses.

When Mr. Chung hurried to the scene, Sammie yelled, "Mr. Chung, Nikki is being mean to me! She pushed me out of line and broke my glasses."

"Is that true, Nikki?" asked Mr. Chung.

"No!" replied Nikki. "Sammie started it. She called me a name and cut in front of me so she could get a drink first."

"No, sir! I was there first," Sammie interrupted.

"You liar! You're always pushing everyone around," yelled Nikki.

"All right, that's enough," a frustrated Mr. Chung broke in. "You girls will have to go to the principal's office to work this one out. I have to get back to class."

Nikki and Sammie are playing a game that will make their conflict worse. In this lesson we will see how this game is played and how we can break free from it.

The Blame Game

Like Nikki and Sammie, we sometimes make choices that lead to conflict. The problem gets worse when we refuse to take responsibility for our choices by playing the blame game. In other words, **the blame game makes conflict worse**. There are five ways people usually play the blame game.

Blame

Blame someone else for your choice.
"My friend made me hit him."
"It's not my fault I talked back to you. You made me mad!"

Cover Up

Cover up what you did wrong in the hope that no one will find out.
"If I can just get this mess cleaned up before Dad gets home, he'll think someone else broke the garage window."

"If I can be really quiet and sneak in the back door, Mom will never know that I got home late."

Make Excuses

Make excuses for doing something wrong or for not doing something right.
"I forgot to do the dishes, Mom."
"I know I said I would make a poster for the school play, but I was just too busy to do it."

Teaching Tip

The examples of playing the blame game can be used as role play activities if desired.

Pretend

Pretend that something you did is not your fault.
"Mom, did you know the lamp in the family room is broken?"
"Is your new CD missing, Dad? Oh, that's too bad."

Lie

Lie about what you did.
"I didn't steal the candy." (But you did.)
"I didn't make the mess in the kitchen." (But you did.)

Playing the Blame Game

Let's look at how Nikki and Sammie could play the blame game in their situation.

Blame Each Other

Sammie: "It's Nikki's fault! She pushed me into the wall and wouldn't let me in line."

Nikki: "It's Sammie's fault! She calls me names and pushes in front of me all the time. If she quits doing that, I'll quit."

Cover Up Their Bad Choice

Both girls: "We'd better not tell Mr. Chung what happened. He'll send us to the principal's office and we'll be in big trouble."

Make Excuses

Sammie: "I was so hot and thirsty after playing soccer. I just wanted to get a drink before I fainted!"

Nikki: "All the kids in line were mad at her for trying to take cuts. They told me to push her away."

Pretend that They Did Nothing Wrong

Both girls: "Problem? No, Mr. Chung, we don't have a problem."

Lie About What They Did

Sammie: "I was just standing in line when Nikki pushed me and told me to get out of her way."

Nikki: "I didn't push Sammie out of line, and I don't know how she got hurt."

The Blame Game Makes Conflict Worse

If Nikki and Sammie develop a habit of playing the blame game, they will convince themselves that their choices were justified. They will try to escape the consequences they deserve. They will believe that their choices are always someone else's fault and they can't change unless other people change first.

The blame game will not solve the girls' problem. Instead the **blame game will make their conflict worse.** God explains what happens to people who play the blame game. "He who conceals his sins does not prosper" (Prov. 28:13).

The blame game is like turning on a lamp and trying to hide its light under a little pillow. You will never succeed in completely hiding the light. In the same way, when you try to hide your wrong or sinful choices, you will never succeed. Even if you fool other people, you will never fool God.

■ **Have you ever played the blame game? In what way? What happened?** (Accept appropriate answers)

■ **Can you please God when you play the blame game? Why not?** (No! God is never pleased when we play the blame game, because it is a form of lying.)

Nikki and Sammie both made wrong choices. It's true that Sammie started the conflict because of her choice to bully Nikki. But Nikki made the choice to respond to Sammie in an angry way. Both girls contributed to the problem and both girls deserve consequences for their individual choices.

■ **Who deserves the consequences if Sammie cuts in front of Nikki and calls her names?** (Sammie. Remember that the person who makes the choice deserves the consequences!)

■ **Who deserves the consequences if Nikki pushed Sammie and called her names?** (Nikki.)

No matter what others do, when you make a bad choice, you deserve a bad consequence. You would be smart to accept that consequence without playing the blame game, so you can avoid getting into double trouble. Let's talk about what that means.

Getting Double Trouble

It is a choice to play the blame game, and this choice has consequences. When you choose to play the blame game, you could find yourself in double trouble. You will probably get a consequence for your bad choice and a consequence for playing the blame game. Let's say you break a lamp in your living room and you tell your parents your brother did it. They find out the truth and give you a consequence for breaking the lamp and a second consequence for lying about it.

In other words, you might get two consequences instead of one. The equation could look like this:

Bad Choice + Blame Game = DOUBLE TROUBLE

Some of the extra consequences you get for playing the blame game will be immediate, while others may be delayed. For example:

● You may be disciplined twice—once for your bad choice and once for playing the blame game.

● Minor conflicts that could have been resolved quickly may grow into major quarrels.

● Relationships may be damaged more severely and be harder to repair.

● Your reputation for playing the blame game will make it hard for people to believe you are innocent, even when you are.

■ **If Nikki and Sammie choose to play the blame game, what kind of double trouble might they face?**

■ **Can you remember a time when you got double trouble?**

As you can tell by now, choosing to play the blame game is not a wise choice and will usually make a conflict worse.

1ST CONSEQUENCE COMING AT YOU FOR PUSHING AND SHOVING

2ND CONSEQUENCE COMING AT YOU FOR PLAYING THE BLAME GAME

Feeling Like a Victim

Another problem occurs when people play the blame game. They often begin to feel like a victim.

■ **What is a victim?** (Someone who is cheated, fooled, or injured by someone else.)

When you are seriously hurt by another's sinful choice, you are a victim and it is right get help. For example, if your home is burglarized, it is right to call the police. But some people think of themselves as victims all the time and believe that all their problems are someone else's fault.

- They blame their family, friends, teachers, or neighbors for their problems, but never themselves.
- They often feel that they are at the mercy of others, and that they have no control over what they do.
- They rarely take responsibility for their contribution to conflicts and problems.
- Their choices are often rooted in self-pity or self-righteousness.
- They master the art of playing the blame game.
- Sadly, they think of themselves as victims all their lives.

Nikki could feel like a victim in her situation, couldn't she? It would be natural for Nikki to think that she is at the mercy of Sammie. She could feel hopeless because she is depending on Sammie to change. She might say, "I'll quit calling her names and pushing her if she quits doing it to me!" The problem here is that Nikki is actually letting Sammie control her. If Sammie doesn't change, then Nikki won't change. Nikki's trapped!

But Nikki doesn't have to feel or act like a victim. There are a number of things that Nikki can do to take responsibility for herself and her choices in this situation, regardless of what Sammie does.

■ **What do you think Nikki could do if Sammie doesn't change?**

Let's explore some ideas.

- Nikki could confess to Sammie that she was wrong to push her and call her names. This would set a good example for Sammie.
- Nikki could ignore Sammie's attempts to bully her, and continue to talk with her friends.
- Without pushing her or striking back, Nikki could refuse to let Sammie take cuts in line.
- Nikki could walk away from Sammie, saying she doesn't want to get into trouble by fighting.
- Nikki could try to explain to Sammie how her choices affect others. She could ask Sammie to leave her alone.
- Nikki could warn Sammie that if she continues to act like a bully, Nikki will report her actions to a teacher, principal, or whoever could help them resolve this problem.

- Nikki could ask Mr. Chung for advice about how she could handle the problem in a right way.

- If the girls were not able to resolve the conflict by themselves, Nikki could ask Mr. Chung if he would mediate. He could help both girls take responsibility for their contribution to the conflict.

- If Nikki thinks Sammie is acting like an enemy, then Nikki could choose to act in a loving way toward her (see Luke 6:27-28). She could invite Sammie to play with her and her friends. This could help Sammie to feel accepted. Sometimes a bully's actions are a way to cover up loneliness or a lack of true friends.

- Nikki could ask her parents to include Sammie on a fun family outing. This could show her how a loving family treats each other. By watching Nikki and her family, Sammie could learn about showing respect to others.

By responding to Sammie in any of these ways, Nikki will be doing all she can to stay out of the victim-trap and on top of the slippery slope. She can depend on the Lord to help her do what is right instead of what she feels like doing. Nikki does not have to wait for Sammie to change before she makes good choices for herself. Nikki can "take charge" of her own responses so that she is not a victim of Sammie's wrong choices.

Resisting the Blame Game

Often you may want other people to change their choices before you change yours. That means that you are putting yourself at the mercy of others. If they don't change, neither will you. You are allowing yourself to feel and act like a victim. You are allowing other people to control your choices. God wants you to control your own choices no matter what others do.

- God wants you to be a victor instead of a victim. The dictionary says that a victor is a winner or a conqueror.

- God wants you to be a victor over your sinful responses toward others.

- God wants you to know the freedom there is in using self-control and in making wise choices that please him.

Not only does God want you to control your choices; as you pray to him, he will give you the power to do so. You can resist feeling and acting like a victim if you choose to do what is right and wise no matter what other people do. That's real freedom!

THE BLAME GAME MAKES CONFLICT WORSE.

Wrapping It Up

God's Word says that those who play the blame game will not prosper even though they may fool themselves and other people for a while. In fact, playing **the blame game makes conflict worse.** However, God promises to forgive those who resist playing the blame game and take responsibility for their choices. Remember the bad news in Proverbs 28:13: "He who conceals his sins does not prosper." The good news is, "He who confesses [admits] and renounces [gives up] them [bad choices] finds mercy [blessings and forgiveness]."

We also learned that we do not need to feel or act like a victim. We can make good choices no matter what anybody else does, and that's freedom!

Closing Prayer

Dear Lord, it seems so easy for me to play the blame game when I make a bad choice. Please forgive me for not accepting responsibility for my own choices. You have shown me that you don't want me to play the blame game. I ask you to change me and give me the power to accept responsibility for my choices without arguing, blaming or making excuses. Thank you, God, for working in me to resist playing the blame game and helping me to do what is right. In Jesus' name,

Amen.

Making It Real

Assign one or more of the suggested activities for Lesson Five in the Activities and Personal Application section of this lesson. Some of the activities are included in Student Activity Book #5.

Activities and Personal Application

Activities one, two, and three can be found in Student Activity Book (SAB) #5.

1. The Blame Game (see SAB 5-8): Use the special game board to practice all of the ways you play the blame game.

2. Super Duper Blame Game Maze (see SAB 5-9): Draw a line from hand to hand along each path to see how many times the blame game just takes you in circles.

3. From Victim to Victor (see SAB 5-10): After reading the relevant Bible passage, indicate whether they acted like victims or victors, and describe what they did. (Answer: they all acted like victors)

4. There are five ways to play the blame game:

- Blame someone else for my choices.
- Cover up what I did wrong.
- Make excuses for my choices.
- Pretend I did nothing wrong.
- Lie about what I did.

List the ways that you play the blame game. What usually happens after you play the blame game? Sometimes you might think that you have fooled people into believing that what you did was not your fault. Who will you never be able to fool? What has God promised to those who try to fool him? (See Gal. 6:7)

5. Teachers, have your class make a collage by drawing scenes of people playing the blame game. Lay out a large piece of butcher paper that has been divided into sections using a marker. There should be one section for each student in your class. Have each student draw or paint an example of a blame game situation in his or her section. Then have them write a brief explanation of their illustrations. Display the collage in the classroom.

6. Variation on Activity Three. Teachers: cut out large puzzle pieces using tag board or cardboard. Give each child a puzzle piece to draw or paint their blame game illustration. Then have the children put the puzzle pieces together.

Dig into the Word

Memory Verse:

Proverbs 28:13

Other Relevant Bible Verses:

2 Samuel 12:1-13
Psalm 32:1-5
1 John 1:9

Applicable Bible Stories:

Assign one or more of the following passages to help children analyze conflict situations in the Bible.

Adam and Eve blaming others (Gen. 3:1-13)

Aaron blaming the people for his sin (Exod. 32:1-24)

Saul blaming his soldiers for his sin (1 Sam. 13:7-12)

The Lesson Summary

Bible Memory Verse

"He who conceals his sins does not prosper, but whoever confesses and renounces them finds mercy" (Prov. 28:13).

Key Principle

The blame game makes conflict worse.

The Main Points of This Lesson

1. Playing the blame game

Playing the blame game is a choice that has consequences.

There are five ways that people play the blame game.

- Blame someone else for your choice.
- Cover up what you did wrong in hopes that no one will find out.
- Make excuses for doing something wrong or not doing something right.
- Pretend that something you did is not your fault.
- Lie about what you did.

2. Getting double trouble

When you make a bad choice and then choose to play the blame game, you may get a consequence for each choice. This is *double trouble.*

Bad choice + Blame game = DOUBLE TROUBLE

3. Feeling like a victim

Playing the blame game can give you an excuse to feel like a victim.

Victims believe that their problems are always someone else's fault.

Playing the blame game makes you feel as if you are at the mercy of other people.

4. Resisting the blame game

God wants you to know that there is freedom in using self-control and in making wise choices that please him.

God wants you to be a victor over your sinful responses toward others by taking control of your own choices no matter what others do.

Whether
you eat
or
drink
or
whatever
you do,
do it all
for the
**glory
of
God.**

1 Corinthians 10:31

Lesson Goal:

To help students learn to view conflict as an opportunity to glorify God, serve other people, and grow to be like Christ.

Lesson Objectives:

By God's grace students will learn to:

1. Glorify God in conflict.
2. Serve other people during conflict.
3. Grow to be more like Christ through conflict..

Key Principle:

Conflict is an opportunity.

Lesson Needs:

Bible
Student Activity Book #6

87

Begin with Prayer

Begin the lesson with prayer that your students will learn to view conflict as an opportunity instead of a problem.

Review and Setting the Stage

- **What are the five ways people play the blame game?** (Blame others for their choices; cover up their choices hoping no one will find out; make excuses for doing wrong or not doing right; pretend they did nothing wrong; or lie about their choices.)

- **Does anyone remember what double trouble is?** (You get a consequence for a bad choice you made and another consequence for playing the blame game instead of taking responsibility for your bad choice.)

- **Why do people who play the blame game often feel like victims?** (Because they feel like they are at the mercy of other people or that other people are controlling them.)

- **What do you think of when you hear the word "conflict"?** (Problem, fight, broken relationships, anger, frustration, hurt, pain, etc.)

Today we are going to learn to think of conflict as an opportunity. Most of us think of conflict as a problem that will always cause pain or embarrassment. But God doesn't see it that way. The Bible teaches that if we handle our differences with other people in a wise way, good things can result. We can please and honor God. We can learn to understand and appreciate other people. And we can grow to be more like Christ.

As we have learned, some conflicts are caused when we make choices to get what we want. The Bible teaches that conflict should never be used as a way to satisfy a selfish desire. Instead, we should understand that **conflict is an opportunity** to show others the power and presence of God as he helps us respond to difficulties in a godly way.

CONFLICT IS AN OPPORTUNITY.

Failing Family Fallout
featuring
NACOMA & MOM

Listen to a story about a girl named Nacoma who has an opportunity to please God in a difficult situation.

As Nacoma sat on her bed, tears streamed down her face. It had been four weeks since her father had told her that he and her mother were going to separate for a while because of problems in their marriage. He assured Nacoma that the separation would only be temporary, but she remembered friends whose parents said the same thing and still got divorced. Her heart was consumed with fear, confusion, and anger. What was she going to do? Suddenly there was a knock at her door.

"Nacoma, may I come in? I want to talk with you," her mother asked as she opened her daughter's bedroom door.

"I hope you're satisfied! You've really done it this time," said Nacoma through her tears. "This is all your fault, Mom. Nag! Nag! Nag! You're always complaining about everything Dad does. In fact, neither one of us can do anything right, according to you! If you didn't nag all the time, Dad would still be here. You wrecked our home!"

"I did not wreck our home! And even if I had tried, I couldn't do it by myself! Your dad isn't perfect, you know! When you are ready to talk about this in a reasonable way, let me know, Nacoma. Until then, I've got better things to do than to stand here and listen to this!" fumed her mother.

"You don't even care about how I feel!" Nacoma cried as her mother left the room.

Nacoma's heart is crushed. Her future looks dark and uncertain. She is lonely and afraid, and she doesn't know what to do. Everything is so mixed up! To whom can she turn for help?

When you are in a painful or difficult situation, there is only one perfectly trustworthy source of help and comfort! GOD! You are not going to understand everything that happens in your life. Sometimes things will seem confusing and hopeless. But to God nothing is confusing or hopeless, and he promises to give you comfort and strength so you can confidently face the difficulties in your life.

Cry out to him and tell him what you're feeling. He understands! Ask him to work in your heart so that you will not be ruled by fear, anger, or any other sinful attitude. Read his Word. It will guide you to do what is right so you don't add more heat to the situation. Seek advice from God's people. Ask those you trust to coach you to respond to your hard times in a wise and godly way.

God Is with You in Conflict

When you are in a conflict, you may feel hopeless and helpless. It may seem as if you are carrying a heavy weight on your shoulders all alone. But the Bible says that God is always with you and he will help you to see conflict as an opportunity instead of a burden. Let's discover three opportunities you have in every conflict.

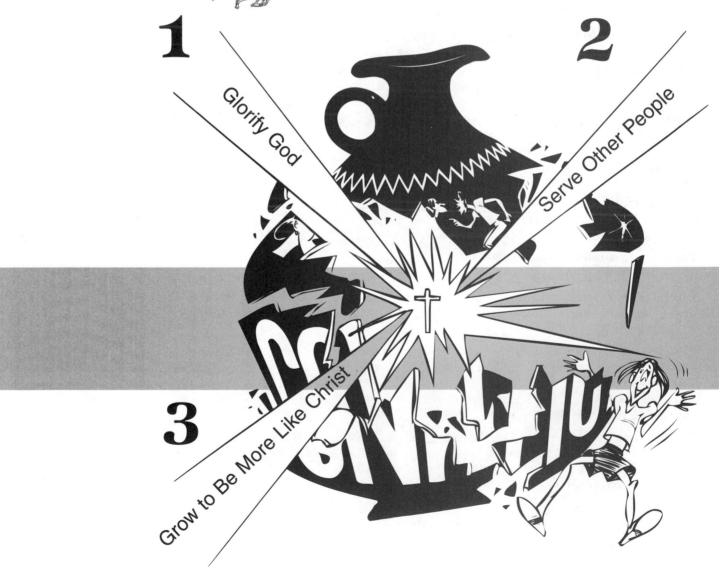

1 Glorify God

2 Serve Other People

3 Grow to Be More Like Christ

Conflict Is an Opportunity

Nacoma could choose to look at the conflict in her family as an enormous burden. If she takes that view, she will probably do things that make the situation worse. She may continue to blame her mother for the separation and increase her feelings of guilt. She could turn against her father and blame him for leaving. Or she might get so angry and afraid that she just withdraws from her parents and refuses to talk to them. None of these attack or escape responses will help to resolve the conflict in Nacoma's family. In fact, they will only make matters worse.

There are two things that will help Nacoma deal with this conflict in a wise way. First, she needs to understand that she is not responsible for how her parents handle their conflicts. She is only responsible for the choices she makes in this situation.

Second, Nacoma needs to resist the temptation to look at the situation as an enormous burden. Of course, it will not be easy for Nacoma to trust God, stop blaming her parents, admit her wrongs, and learn to share her feelings respectfully. In spite of these challenges, the Bible says that

Nacoma should look at the conflict in her family in a positive way. When the Apostle Paul was teaching the early Christians how to deal with conflicts over what they should eat and drink, he said this:

"So whether you eat or drink or whatever you do, do it all for the glory of God. Do not cause anyone to stumble, whether Jews, Greeks or the church of God—even as I try to please everyone in every way. For I am not seeking my own good but the good of many, so that they may be saved. Follow my example, as I follow the example of Christ" (1 Cor. 10:31-11:1).

Paul was telling the Christians not to get worried and upset about their conflicts. Instead, they should see that conflict always provides three opportunities to do good things. First, whenever we are in conflict, we can find ways to glorify God. Second, we should look for ways to serve other people. And third, we can cooperate with God as he uses conflict to help us grow to be more like Jesus. These three opportunities are present in every conflict situation—both for Nacoma and for you! Let's look at them more carefully.

Glorify God in Conflict

To *glorify God* means that you will show God honor and bring him praise. You can do this even when you are in a conflict! First, you can believe that he works in *all* kinds of situations to bring about his good purposes. Then you can make wise-way choices to show God that you love, respect, and trust him. This can help to show other people that God is loving, wise, and faithful. You might be thinking, "That sounds good, but how can I do that when I'm in a conflict?" Let me suggest three ways you can glorify God.

Trust God

You can glorify God by believing and trusting what his Word says. Psalm 145 says he always keeps his promises and he is always faithful. Believing this will help you to resist the temptation to blame God for your problems or to respond to them in a sinful way,

like running away or attacking others. Instead of following your own ideas and feelings, you can trust in God's promises and cooperate with him to do what is right. This will please and honor God (see Ps. 28:7; Prov. 3:5; Matt. 22: 37-39; Luke 6:27-31; Phil. 2:4).

Obey God

You can also glorify God by obeying his commands, even when you are in conflict. Rather than attacking others, you can choose to love and serve them. Even when others attack you, you can choose to stay on top of the slippery slope. You can obey God's by overlooking small offenses and by confronting serious concerns respectfully.

Instead of playing the blame game or becoming angry and bitter, you can obey God by confessing your wrongs and forgiving others. This obedience will also glorify God (see Mark 10:45; Luke 6:27-28; John 14:15; Rom. 12:19-21; Eph. 4:29; Eph. 6:1-3; James 4:6-8; 1 Peter 2:21-23).

Imitate God

Finally, you can glorify God as you imitate his character, especially in conflict situations. Remember, you were created in his image and he wants you to act like him. He is loving, patient, gentle, and forgiving. He doesn't treat us as our sins deserve.

"The Lord is compassionate and gracious, slow to anger, abounding in love. He will not always accuse, nor will he harbor his anger forever; he does not treat us as our sins deserve or repay us according to our iniquities" (Psalm 103:8-10).

Jesus says we should treat others the same way, even when they don't deserve it (see Luke 6:27). When you respond to people this way, you will imitate and glorify God (see Eph. 5:1-2; 1 John. 2:6).

It is important to realize that when you are in a conflict you will always glorify something. In other words, you will always treat something as being very big. You can focus all of your attention on your problems, your fears, or even on your enemies, and make them look overwhelming. On the other hand, you can focus your attention on God and the promises he makes to take care of you. This will help to show others how big God really is. In particular, you can choose to:

- Show God that you love him and trust his Word.
- Willingly obey him even if you don't feel like it.
- Imitate him by being patient, kind, merciful, and loving.

When you see that **conflict is an opportunity** and make these choices, you will show other people that God is real and that he is the one who is helping you to do what is right.

■ **How can Nacoma glorify God in this situation?**

With God's help, Nacoma can refuse to let fear and anger control her choices. Instead, she can depend on God's Word and his promises, and trust him to work in her parents according to his plan. This will help her to resist the temptation to try to control her parents. Nacoma can pray for strength to obey God's command to treat her mother and father with respect, even when their choices hurt her (Eph. 6:1-2). She can talk to them in a loving way (Eph. 4:15) and resist the temptation to gossip about them (Prov. 26:20). She can even seek godly advisors who can listen to her struggles and coach her to respond to this situation in a way that will please God and help her parents (see Prov. 12:15; Prov. 15:21-23). Most of all, Nacoma can pray for her parents, asking God to help them to be peacemakers and to reconcile their marriage.

All of these things will please and honor God and bring him glory.

Serve Other People During Conflict

Conflict doesn't usually bring out the best in you, does it? When you are having a dispute with someone, it is easy to give in to your sinful heart and become angry, bitter, and mean. Thoughts of retaliation, instead of plans for reconciliation, often fill your mind. Your friends who do not know Jesus will tell you to "look out for yourself." But Jesus says something different. In Luke 6:27-28, he says, "Love your enemies, do good to those who hate you, bless those who curse you, pray for those who mistreat you." In other words, **conflict is an opportunity** to serve other people by doing what is good and right. Jesus teaches several ways that you can do this.

Love

To act in a *loving way* toward a person who has been mean and hurtful to you pleases God and blesses others. You can do this by speaking and acting with kindness, patience, and self-control toward others, even if they are unkind to you.

Do Good

At times people may treat you badly because of something you have done or because of problems in their lives. This is an opportunity for you *to do good* things for them, such as helping them with their problems or confronting them in a loving way. This will be a witness to others of the power and presence of God in your life.

Bless

To bless others in conflict means that you will *speak kindly to them and about them*. You have the opportunity to please God by saying things to encourage people who have said mean things to you.

Pray

This is a very powerful response to conflict. It's good for those who cause you pain, and it's good for you. When you pray for those who mistreat you, you will be less likely to slide down the slippery slope. You can pray that God will bless them, work in their hearts, and help them do what is right. You can also ask him to help you love them, do good to them, and bless them.

When you are in conflict, you can serve not only the person who is opposing you but also the people who are watching what you do. As you choose to act in a loving and self-controlled way, you can be a Christ-like example to them and show them how they can stay on top of the slippery slope. What a great way to encourage and serve others!

■ **How could Nacoma serve her parents?**

Nacoma would need to talk to the Lord about her feelings of fear, anger, and confusion. Her only hope is to depend on him to help her do what is right and good regardless of her circumstances or feelings. Nacoma should confess to her mother that she was wrong to be so disrespectful toward her and blame her for the breakdown in the marriage. Nacoma could pray that God will give her a loving heart toward her mother and father. She can express her feelings and concerns to them in a gentle and loving way. The way she speaks can bless her parents even if she needs to say hard things. She could encourage them to trust God and obey his Word. She could pray that God would bring healing to her parents' relationship and strengthen their marriage. She could offer to help her parents with their household chores so that they would have more time to work out their difficulties. And if she has brothers and sisters, she could set a good example for them and help them to respond constructively to this situation.

> **Role Play Activity:** You have just heard that a new boy in the neighborhood is saying mean things about you. You are not sure why he has decided to pick on you. Act out how you could glorify God and serve this boy.

Grow to Be More Like Christ

The highest goal God has for his children is for us to become like his Son (see Rom. 8:28-29). In other words, God wants us to become like Jesus in the way we think, speak, and act. Let's look at some ways you can grow to be like Christ.

Recognize Your Need for God

God wants you to become like Jesus, and he will provide ways for that to happen. He may bring situations into your life that show your weakness and your need for him (see 1 Cor. 12:9-10).

When you are in conflict and ask for his help, the Holy Spirit will give you the power to make godly decisions. The more you depend on Jesus, the more you will be like him!

Confess Your Sin

God will often use conflict to uncover what is in your heart—things like pride, anger, bitterness, and unforgiveness. When this happens, you can confess those sins, receive forgiveness from God,

and ask God to help you change and become more like Jesus (see 1 John 1:9). You can also ask for forgiveness from any others you have offended. We will discuss this in more detail in later chapters.

Practice New Attitudes and Actions

When athletes are going to compete in the Olympics, they need to practice many hours a day to develop skills in their particular sport. Part of their training will include overcoming bad habits and developing good habits so they can become the best in their sport. In the same way, you will grow to be like Christ as you begin to practice new and godly habits in conflict situations. For example, when people provoke or frus-

trate you, you can practice love and forgiveness. When they are slow to respond to your needs or desires, you can practice patience. When they attack you or your ideas, you can practice self-control. As God gives you strength to be like his Son, you will experience many blessings that come from a Christ-like heart and mind (see 1 Cor. 4:13; Gal. 5:22-23; and 1 Peter 2:21-24).

■ **How can Nacoma grow to be more like Jesus?**

Nacoma can admit that she is powerless to change her parents or their situation. She can talk to the Lord about it, thanking him that he does have the power to change people and situations. With God's help, she can read and memorize Bible passages that will help her imitate Jesus. When she makes disobedient or disrespectful choices toward either of her parents, she can confess her sin and ask their forgiveness. She may also need to confess to the Lord that she has given in to fear and worry, and she hasn't trusted him to care for her family. Finally, she can pray that God will help her practice new attitudes and choices that reflect Jesus—like being loving, kind, patient, forgiving, respectful, and obedient toward her father and mother.

With God There Is Help and Hope

When we are in difficult situations, we can give in to fear and hopelessness, or we can run to God, who is called our "strong tower" in Proverbs 18:10. He is "our refuge and strength, an ever-present help in trouble," according to Psalm 46:1. It is God's desire that we call on him for help, and he will hear our voices, says Psalm 116:1-6.

If you are ever in a situation like the one Nacoma is facing, it would be easy for you to think that you are the only one who can rescue your family from the pain they are experiencing. You might feel guilty and responsible for your parents' problems. You might try to manipulate or control your parents to keep them from making certain choices. You will probably discover that this is a useless effort. You have no power to "fix" your parents. In fact, you need to be prepared for the fact that no matter what you do, your parents may still decide to do things you don't like.

Just as our choices belong to us, our parent's choices belong to them. They are responsible for decisions they make. You can pray for your parents. You can ask people you trust for advice about how to respond to your parents' problems in a wise way. You can even ask others to try to persuade your parents to get help with their difficulties. But mostly, you need to trust God to take care of your parents and your family. With God, there is help and hope in the most difficult conflicts. No matter what happens, God has promised always to be with you and watch over you.

When we are directly or indirectly involved in a conflict, our responsibility before God is to take the opportunity to *glorify him*, *serve other people*, and *grow to be like Christ*. And with God's help, we can do just that.

Wrapping It Up

In this lesson we have learned to see that **conflict is an opportunity** to do three things: *glorify God, serve other people,* and *grow to be like Christ.* We glorify God when we trust him, obey him and imitate him in all we do and say, even when we are in conflict. We have discovered that God is pleased when we serve other people in conflict situations, both those with whom we are having a conflict and those who are watching us. We can serve other people by loving them, doing good for them, blessing them, and praying for them. This demonstrates God's power and presence in our lives.

We have also learned that the process of growing to be more like Christ starts with recognizing that we are weak and powerless. As we depend on God's strength, we can do what is right. We can confess our sins and be forgiven by God and seek forgiveness from others. And we must practice godly attitudes and habits at all times. We need to think, say, and do what pleases God.

As we view and respond to **conflict as an opportunity,** we will understand and experience God's promise in Matthew 5:9, "Blessed are the peacemakers: for they shall be called children of God" (KJV).

Closing Prayer

Dear Lord, help me to see my conflicts as opportunities to glorify you, serve other people, and grow to be like Jesus. Please forgive me for giving in to fear and sinful desires when I am in a conflict. Please help me to remember that you do not want me to control other people's choices, just my own. I want to remember that I am powerless, but you are powerful. You have promised to give me strength to do things that please you. Help me to think godly thoughts, say only things that build people up, and do what is good and right. Help me to be a peacemaker. In Jesus' name,

Amen.

Making It Real

Assign one or more of the suggested activities for Lesson Six that are found in the Activities and Personal Application section of this lesson. Some of the activities are included in Student Activity Book #6.

Activities and Personal Application

Activities one and two can be found in Student Activity Book (SAB) #6.

1. Untangling the Opportunity (see SAB 6-9): Practice finding the opportunities in conflict by unscrambling the words on the right, drawing a line to the phrase they complete on the left, and writing the appropriate word into the blank. (Answers: 1-Practice 2-Serve 3-Bless 4-Confess 5-Recognize 6-Glorify 7-Pray 8-Grow 9-Imitate 10-Trust 11-Obey 12-Love 13-Good)

2. The Worse It Is the Better It is (see SAB 6-10): Read the passages and then describe how people brought praise and honor to God by trusting, obeying, or imitating him in difficult situations.

3. Read the story of Joseph in Genesis 37 and 39-50 with your parents or teacher. In each chapter make note of all the things that Joseph did that would glorify God and serve other people.

4. This week make a list of some times that you chose to please yourself and some times that your choices pleased the Lord.

5. Are you having a conflict with someone now? If so, make a list of things you can do with God's help to glorify him, serve other people, and grow to be like Jesus in this situation.

Dig into the Word

Memory Verses:

1 Corinthians 10:31

Other Relevant Bible Verses:

Romans 1:21
Romans 4:20-21
Romans 15:5-6
Romans 15:17
Philippians 2:1-18
2 Thessalonians 1:11-12
1 Peter 2:12

Applicable Bible Stories:

Assign one or more of the following passages to help children analyze conflict situations in the Bible.

David spares Saul's life (1 Samuel 24:1-22)

Daniel in the lion's den (Dan. 6:1-28)

Peter addresses the crowd at Pentecost (Acts 2:14-41)

Stephen's speech to the Sanhedrin and his stoning (Acts 6:8-8:1)

Paul and Silas in prison (Acts 16:16-40)

The Lesson Summary

Bible Memory Verse

"So whether you eat or drink whatever you do, do it all for the glory of God" (1 Cor. 10:31).

Key Principle

Conflict is an opportunity.

The Main Points of This Lesson

1. Glorify God in conflict.

Trust God to carry out his plan.
Obey God's commands found in the Bible.
Imitate God's character, which is loving, kind, patient, and forgiving.

2. Serve other people during conflict.

Love your enemies.
Do good to those who hate you.
Bless those who curse you.
Pray for those who mistreat you (Luke 6:26-27).

3. Grow to be more like Christ through conflict.

Recognize your need for God.
Confess your sins and receive forgiveness from God. Seek forgiveness from those you have offended.
Practice new habits regarding what you think, what you say, and what you do.

Lesson 7 — The Five A's for Resolving Conflict

> If we **confess** our sins, he is faithful and just and will **forgive** us our sins and purify us from all unrighteousness.
>
> 1 John 1:9

Lesson Goal:

To help students understand how to respond to conflict in a biblically faithful manner.

Lesson Objective:

By God's grace students will learn:
1. What the 5A's are and how to use them.
2. What the biblical principles of repentance and confession are.

Key Principle:

The 5A's can resolve conflict.

Lesson Needs:

Bible
Student Activity Book #7
Worksheet Three—Using the 5A's (Appendix C)

Begin with Prayer

Begin the lesson with prayer that your students will understand the importance of repentance, confession, and forgiveness as it relates to conflict situations in their lives. Pray that they will apply the 5A's to resolve their conflicts.

Also, remember to discuss or collect any homework assignments you may have given to your students.

Review and Setting the Stage

During the last lesson we learned that when we are in conflict, we have three opportunities.

■ **What are the three opportunities in every conflict situation?** (Glorify God, serve other people, and grow to be like Christ.)

■ **How can you glorify God in conflict?** (Trust, obey, and imitate.)

■ **How can you serve others in conflict?** (Love your enemies, do good to those who hate you, bless those who curse you, and pray for those who mistreat you.)

■ **How can you grow to be more like Jesus when you are in a conflict?** (Recognize your need for God, confess your sin, and practice new attitudes and actions.)

Conflict provides opportunities to obey the Lord in difficult situations when everything in you wants do just the opposite. One of the hardest things to do is to "get the log out of your own eye" by admitting that you have done something wrong. I know that this is true, because it's hard for me to admit when I've done something wrong. I try to convince myself that playing the blame game is okay. But the Bible says that God wants us to confess our sinful choices. We please and glorify him when we do! We also receive the benefit of confession—he promises to forgive us. "If we confess our sins, he is faithful and just and will forgive us our sins and purify us from all unrighteousness" (1 John 1:9).

Teaching Tip

The story could be used as a role play activity.

Pointless Put-Downs
featuring
CONNIE & NIKKI

Speech bubbles: "NIKKI COULDN'T HIT OR CATCH ANYTHING LAST NIGHT!" / "I'M NOT SURE SHE EVEN KNEW WE WERE PLAYING A GAME!"

Listen to a story about two friends who got into a conflict and then played the blame game.

Nikki and Connie are usually very good friends, but today they are not speaking to each other. They had a fight on the playground and both of them are feeling hurt and angry. Connie had announced to everyone that it was Nikki's fault that their softball team lost the game the night before. "She couldn't hit or catch anything last night," laughed Connie. "I'm not sure if she even knew we were playing a game."

Then Nikki retaliated by making fun of Connie's low grades on weekly spelling tests. "Connie even has to check her own nametag so she can spell her name right," Nikki retorted.

The fight divided Miss Johnson's class as the students sided with either Nikki or Connie. When Miss Johnson tried to find out what happened to create such a conflict, Nikki and Connie blamed each other for the problem.

■ **What choices did Nikki and Connie make to create this conflict?** (Connie made fun of Nikki about softball; Nikki ridiculed Connie about her low grades in spelling; the girls stopped speaking to each other.)

■ **What do you think is at the root of this conflict?** (Each girl's pride was hurt; both were afraid of what others might think of them; both wanted approval not criticism; neither of them wanted to take responsibility for their own poor performance in baseball or spelling.)

Nikki and Connie could have handled this situation in a different way—one that could have resolved the conflict.

■ **What does it mean to "resolve a conflict"?** (To find an answer to the problem; to settle the conflict; to be friends again.)

As we've already seen, it's not easy to resolve a conflict. We often play the blame game, which makes conflicts worse. Today we will look at something that is just the opposite of the blame game. It's called the 5A's. **The 5A's can resolve conflict** and help you bring glory to God .

5A's

1. **AD-MIT**
I'M IT.
BROKE THE BOND
THAT'S TIGHTLY FIT.

2. **A-POL-O-GIZE**
TELL NO LIES.
I HURT YOU, I RECOGNIZE.

3. **AC-CEPT**
GLADLY KEPT
A CONSEQUENCE
I WON'T FORGET.

4. **ASK** YOU
'FORE WE'RE THROUGH.
FORGIVENESS—WHAT I NEED
FROM YOU.

5. **ALTER** NOW
THIS IS HOW:
"GOD,
CHANGE MY HEART.
PLEASE DO IT NOW!"

102

Using the 5A's

If you are going to respond to a conflict in a way that pleases God, you need to apply his principles of *repentance, confession, and forgiveness.* Let me define these terms for you.

- Repentance: You understand that you have made a sinful choice; you are willing to take responsibility for it; and you have a desire in your heart to change.
- Confession: You admit openly and honestly to the Lord and to all the people you have hurt or offended that you know your choice was sinful and wrong.
- Forgiveness: You make a promise not to hold a person's sins against him or her. In other words, you forgive as God forgives you.

These three principles are the foundation of the 5A's, which is a process you can use to respond to your conflicts according to God's Word.

The First "A" Is to Admit

The first "A" is to *admit* what you did wrong.

This means that you take responsibility for your sinful choices, as well as the sinful roots of those choices. The Bible calls this *confession.*

It will be natural for you to think that other people's wrongs are worse than yours and that they need to admit their wrongs first. But this is not what Jesus says. In Matthew 7:3-5 he says, "Why do you look at the speck of sawdust in your brother's eye and pay no attention to the plank in your own eye?...You hypocrite, first take the plank out of your own eye, and then you will see clearly to remove the speck from your brother's eye." Jesus wants you to admit your wrongs first, even if you think they are smaller than other people's wrongs.

Admitting is the first step toward resolving your conflicts. You must admit your sins (both your attitudes and actions) to God and then to everyone involved in the conflict. An effective way to admit is to use words like these:

- "I admit I was wrong when I (name your specific sinful attitude and bad choice)."
- "I admit I was angry and disrespectful, and I was wrong to talk back to you."
- "I admit I was wrong and selfish when I left you out of the group. I was jealous because my friends seemed to like you better than me."

The words "I admit I was wrong" demonstrate that you are taking ownership or responsibility for your attitudes and your choices.

■ **Can you think of other examples?**

"I admit I was wrong when . . ."

The Second "A" Is to Apologize

The second "A" is to *apologize* for how your choice affected someone else.

When you apologize for the effect your choice had on someone, you tell the person how sorry you are for hurting him or her. You could say something like this:

- "I am sorry for (acknowledge how you may have affected the person)."
- "I am sorry for hurting your feelings."
- "I am sorry for embarrassing you in front of your friends."

■ **Can you think of other examples?**

- "I am sorry for . . . you."

Some people think that when they admit to and apologize for their bad choices, it's like saying the fault was all theirs and the other person did nothing wrong. This is not true. The other person's choices are not your responsibility—only your choices are! And God wants each of you to admit and apologize only for your own choices. Admitting and apologizing does not cancel the other person's wrong choices. Admitting and apologizing demonstrates that you are taking responsibility for your own choices, and that you are sorry for those choices.

It is important to understand that there is a difference between worldly sorrow, which is being sorry for getting caught, and godly sorrow, which is being sorry for doing wrong. "Godly sorrow brings repentance that leads to salvation and leaves no regret, but worldly sorrow brings death" (2 Cor. 7:10).

When you are sorry only for getting caught, you will probably make the same choices in the future; you will just be more careful not to get caught again. This can lead to dishonesty, deceit, and much more trouble.

However, when you realize that you have done wrong and feel genuine sorrow or regret, you will want to change your choices. The Bible calls this *repentance.* You will take responsibility for the effect your choice had on others, and you will want to resist the temptation to make the same wrong choices in the future. This doesn't mean that you will become perfect; you may still struggle with the same wrong choices, especially if those choices are habits. Repentance means that you will ask God to help you to conquer your wrong choices and give you the determination to make right choices more often. God will do his good work in you, as the Bible promises: "He who began a good work in you will carry it on to completion until the day of Christ Jesus" (Phil. 1:6).

Be sure that you don't admit to or apologize for choices that you did not make. Friends may try to persuade you to take the blame for choices they have made. It's important to take responsibility for your own choices, but not for anyone else's.

Role Play Activity: You and your sister get into an argument over whose turn it is to clean up the kitchen after dinner. You both say hurtful things to each other and accuse each other of being lazy. Using the first two A's, demonstrate how you can handle the conflict.

The Third "A" Is to Accept

The third "A" is to *accept the consequences* for your choices.

An important and necessary part of resolving conflict is accepting the consequences for choices. When you accept your consequences without arguing or pouting, you demonstrate that your repentance is genuine. In other words, you are truly sorry for what you did, and you want to make it right. For example, if you admit that you broke a window, you should offer to pay for a new one. By doing this, you are showing that:

- You are sorry for doing wrong, instead of just being sorry for getting caught.
- You are taking responsibility for your choices, and by doing so, you are glorifying the Lord.
- You are resisting the temptation to blame someone else for your choices.
- You are not trying to get out of the consequences, but rather you are accepting your consequence of making restitution for what you did.

Sometimes we think that when we admit, apologize, and ask for forgiveness we should automatically be released from the consequences for our choices. This is not true. While some people may be merciful and release us from the consequences,

they do not have to do so. We always need to be prepared to accept the consequences of our actions.

Here are some things that you can say to show that you are accepting your consequences:

- "I understand why I need to (describe the consequences you need to accept)."
- "I understand why I need to stay home from the game tonight."
- "I understand why I need to get a zero on my math test, since I cheated."

■ **Can you think of other examples?**

- "I understand why I need to . . . "

This is not to say that you will like the consequences, but rather that you are willing to accept them because you know that they are a result of your choices.

The Fourth "A" Is to Ask

The fourth "A" is to *ask for forgiveness* from the Lord and the people you sinned against.

At this point you are seeking forgiveness from God and from those you have hurt or offended. Once you honestly admit your sins, God will always forgive you, and other people usually will, too. Sometimes the person you wronged will quickly say, "I forgive you." But if not, you may need to ask this question: "Will you please forgive me?"

If you see that the person is having trouble forgiving you, you may need to ask yourself if you have confessed and apologized sincerely and completely. If you haven't, try again and this time make your confession sincere. If you have, then wait patiently and resist the temptation to pressure the person to forgive you. In the meantime, you can thank God that he has forgiven you and pray that he will soften the person's heart so that he or she will forgive you, too. You can make a choice to treat the person in a respectful and kind way.

Even though we'll talk about forgiveness in more detail in the next lesson, I want to briefly explain what the words "I forgive you" mean according to the Bible. The person giving forgiveness makes a commitment to forgive as Jesus forgives. When Jesus forgives, he forgives completely. He harbors no bitterness or resentment in his heart, and he promises to give us a new beginning in our relationship with him.

If you have taken responsibility for your sinful choices by using the first three "A's," then you have made it easier for the person you hurt to forgive you. When you ask for forgiveness, you are seeking to restore your relationship. You are seeking reconciliation.

The Fifth "A" Is to Alter

The fifth "A" is to *alter your choices* in the future.

When you alter choices, it means you change your bad choices to good choices in the future. In other words, instead of making the same bad choices over and over, you can begin to think and plan what to do differently the next time. You should tell others how you want to change, and pray that God will give you the heart and the will to do so. This is further evidence of *repentance.*

Webster's dictionary defines *alter* as "to make or become different." This definition sheds light on what it means to alter your choices. When you sin by making a wrong choice, you need to learn to make different choices in the future. It's like turning and going in a different direction. For example, instead of coming home late, you can come home on time, even if you are having fun at your friend's house and want to stay longer. Using the "fifth A," you can explain what you plan to do differently the next time by saying something like:

- "With God's help, next time I will . . . (explain what you plan to do differently) instead of . . . (name the bad choice you made)."
- "With God's help, next time I will ask for permission to say out later instead of choosing not to come home on time."

■ **Can you think of other examples?**

● "With God's help, next time I will . . . instead of . . . "

Altering a choice can be difficult, especially if your choice has become a habit. Don't get discouraged or give up hope. God can change your heart and help you change your choices from wrong to right. In other words, for a Christian it's never too late to start doing what's right.

106

Let's talk about how Nikki and Connie can please the Lord and stay on top of the slippery slope by using the 5A's to resolve their conflict.

Connie could say to Nikki:

First A: "I admit I was wrong to make fun of you about the game last night. I wanted to show off for our friends."

Second A: "I am sorry for embarrassing you in front of the kids at school."

Third A: "I know that what I did was wrong and I need to tell the whole class that I shouldn't have teased you like I did."

Fourth A: "Will you please forgive me?"

Fifth A: "With God's help, next time I will not laugh at you when you make mistakes in softball. I'll try to encourage you instead."

■ **How was Connie's admission? Very good, wasn't it?**

At this point, Nikki would need to say to Connie, "I forgive you." Nikki would also need to use the 5A's to confess that she was wrong to tease Connie about her low spelling grades. If Connie forgives Nikki, the reconciliation process will be complete and the girls will be friends again. No wall of conflict will stand between them.

■ **Does Connie need to admit only to Nikki that she was wrong?** (No.)

■ **Who else does she need to talk to?** (Miss Johnson and the fifth grade class)

Using the 5A's, write out an admission that Connie could give to Miss Johnson and the class.

First A: "I admit I was wrong when I _____ ."

Second A: "I am sorry for _____ ."

Third A: "I understand why _____ ."

Fourth A: "Will you please forgive me?"

Fifth A: "With God's help, next time I will _____ ."

As Nikki and Connie use the 5A's to resolve their conflict, they will be able to stay on top of the slippery slope. Their friendship will be restored, and they will please God through their obedience. In addition, their good example may help their friends see how to break free from the blame game and quickly admit their wrong choices. Choosing to use the 5A's can produce many good consequences!

THE 5A'S CAN RESOLVE CONFLICT.

Role Play Activity: Your mother sends you to the store for a few groceries. She gives you enough money to get a candy bar for yourself, too. On your way to the market, you pass an ice cream parlor, and give in to the temptation to go inside and order a banana split. After paying, you don't have enough money for the groceries for your mother. Use the 5A's to handle this situation properly.

Wrapping It Up

When you are in a conflict, you have a choice to respond either by using the 5A's or by playing the blame game. As we have learned, playing the blame game will make the conflict worse. There are no benefits to playing the blame game, but there are many benefits to using the 5A's. **The 5A's can resolve conflict.** By using the 5A's you can:

- Obey God by getting the log out of your own eye (Matt. 7:5).

- Have happier, healthier and stronger friendships.

- Feel confident that you are resolving conflict God's way.

- Glorify God, serve others, and grow to be like Christ—which always pleases him!

You can depend on God to help you take responsibility for your choices by using the 5A's. He is faithful and he is with you! Let's pray right now.

Closing Prayer

Dear Lord, sometimes it is hard for me to admit that I do things wrong. Please forgive me for my pride and my unwillingness to accept responsibility for my choices. Please help me to repent and see my sins more honestly. Make me willing to confess that I have contributed to conflicts by what I have said and what I have done. Help me use the 5A's to resolve the conflicts in my life, and help me to seek and give forgiveness for your sake. In Jesus' name,
Amen.

Making It Real

Assign one or more of the suggested activities for Lesson 7 in the Activities and Personal Application section of this lesson. Some of the activities are included in Student Activity Book #7.

The Gospel for Kids

The apostle Paul is a good example of someone who changed wrong choices to right ones. At one time, he chose to treat Christians in a harsh and cruel way. Then God changed his heart and called him to be a Christian. Paul altered or changed his choices and began to teach the truth about Jesus to people in many countries (Acts 9:1-20).

It's important to realize that before Paul's choices changed, his heart was changed. God opened Paul's eyes to see that he needed to know Jesus as his Savior before God would help him to alter his choices. In the same way, you need to know Jesus as *your* Savior before you can depend on him to help you alter your choices!

■ **Do you know Jesus as *your* Savior?** If you would like to know Jesus as your Savior, you need to:

Admit to him that you are a sinner. "For all have sinned and fall short of the glory of God" (Rom. 3:23).

Believe that Jesus is God's Son and that he died and was brought back to life so that your sins would be forgiven. "Believe that Jesus is the Christ, the Son of God, and that by believing you may have life in his name" (John 20:31).

Ask Jesus to forgive your sins, and then *receive* his gift of salvation. "Yet to all who received him, to those who believed in his name, he gave the right to become children of God" (John 1:12).

If you want to receive Jesus as your Savior, you can pray the prayer below.

Salvation Prayer

Lord, I admit that I have sinned against you in my heart and with my choices. I have been disobedient and disrespectful to you and to lots of other people. I am so sorry for living to please myself. I know I deserve to be punished, but I believe that you died on the cross to save me from my sins. I ask you to come into my heart and help me to love, obey, and serve you all the days of my life. In Jesus' name,

Amen.

Teaching Tip

This section may be used now or later depending on time limitations. The 5A's is a great way to teach students about salvation as well as reconciliation. This process will guide them as they confess their sins to the Lord, receive his forgiveness, and ask for the free gift of salvation through Christ. (A Student Activity Sheet is available to guide students through this process.)

Teaching Tip

Teachers, feel free to expand on the gospel message presented here. Some students in your class may never have heard it before, while others may be quite familiar with it.

Once you take these steps to admit, believe, and ask, you can depend on the living God to be with you and work in you to help you make necessary changes in your choices. This will not happen all at once, but day by day God will help you learn how to make choices that are right in his eyes.

Activities and Personal Application

Activities one and two can be found in Student Activity Book (SAB) #7.

1. Word Find (see SAB 7-9): Find the 5A words in the puzzle.

2. Practice Makes Perfect (see SAB 7-10): Using the 5A's as a guide, write a confession for each of the situations.

3. Think of a choice that you have made that has contributed to a conflict with someone in your life. Use the 5A's Worksheet to write out your confession.

4. Write a play about a conflict, and use the 5A's to resolve that conflict. Be creative! You will need to decide what type of conflict to resolve.

Then set the scene and develop the story.

- Write the play.
- Assign parts.
- Rehearse the play.
- Develop costumes.
- Make programs.
- Choose ushers and stage help.
- Decide if you want to videotape the play and who will do it.
- Set a date to act out the play for your parents and guests.
- Perform your play.

This can be done as a class, group, or individually—with help and guidance from an adult, of course!

Dig into the Word

Memory Verse:

1 John 1:9

Other Relevant Bible Verses:

Psalm 32
Psalm 51
Proverbs 28:13
James 5:16

Applicable Bible Stories:

Assign one or more of the following passages to help students analyze conflict situations in the Bible.

The Ninevites repenting (Jonah 3:6-9)

The prodigal son and the forgiving father (Luke 15:11-24)

Zacchaeus pays restitution (Luke 19: 1-10)

The Lesson Summary

Bible Memory Verse

"If we confess our sins, he is faithful and just and will forgive us our sins and purify us from all unrighteousness" (1 John 1:9).

Key Principle

The 5A's can resolve conflict.

The Main Points of This Lesson

1.

The 5A's for resolving conflict

The 5A's are steps that you can use to respond to your conflicts according to God's Word.

Three principles are the foundation of the 5A's:

- Repentance: You understand that you have make a sinful choice; you are willing to take responsibility for it; and you have a desire in your heart to change.

- Confession: You admit openly and honestly to the Lord and to all the people you hurt or offended that you know your choice was sinful and wrong.

- Forgiveness: You make a promise not to hold a person's sins against him or her. In other words, you forgive as Jesus forgives you.

To resolve a conflict between you and another person, you need to take responsibility for your choices, settle the conflict, and restore your relationship. *The 5A's* will help you do that.

The 5A's are *the opposite* of the blame game.

You take responsibility for your choices when you use *the 5A's.*

- First A: *Admit* what you did wrong.
- Second A: *Apologize* for how your choice affected the person.
- Third A: *Accept* the consequences for your choice.
- Fourth A: *Ask* for forgiveness.
- Fifth A: *Alter* your choice in the future.

God wants you to admit *one hundred percent* of your responsibility for your choices. When you offer to replace something that you broke, you are accepting the consequences of your choices. This is called *making restitution*.

2.

Biblical principles of repentance and confession

After you have made a sinful choice, you need to *admit (confess)* to God and to the person you sinned against.

Being sorry for getting caught is *worldly sorrow* and is not a sign of repentance.

Being sorry for doing wrong is *godly sorrow* and is a sign of repentance.

With God's help, you can *alter* your choices from bad to good.

The Freedom of Forgiveness

Be kind and compassionate to one another, **forgiving each other,** just as in Christ **God forgave you.**

Ephesians 4:32

Lesson Goal:

To help students understand the importance of forgiveness.

Lesson Objectives:

By God's grace students will learn:

1. What forgiveness is not.
2. The four promises of forgiveness.
3. The importance of seeking and giving forgiveness.
4. When to give forgiveness.
5. How to express forgiveness.
6. Why they should forgive others.

Key Principle:

Forgiveness is a choice.

Lesson Needs:

Bible
Student Activity Book #8

Begin with Prayer

Begin the lesson with prayer that your students will understand the importance of seeking and giving forgiveness to the glory of God.

Note to Teachers

Someone once asked me, "What does forgiveness have to do with conflict resolution?" My answer was, "It is the heartbeat of conflict resolution. Without it, you don't have conflict resolution." When the Lord commands us to go and be reconciled (Matt. 5:24), he means that we are to seek and give forgiveness so that our relationships can be restored. Since we have been completely forgiven in Christ, we should be the most forgiving people in the world. We are to forgive just as the Lord forgives us!

Review and Setting the Stage

- **Who can list the 5A's in order?** (Admit; Apologize; Accept the consequences; Ask for forgiveness; Alter your choices.)

- **Does anyone remember what confession means?** (Admitting sinful choices and apologizing for how they affected someone.)

- **Does anyone remember what repentance means?** (Realizing I have done wrong, then wanting to change the way I think and act from bad to good with God's help.)

Very good! Those are important words to remember.

- **Do you know what God promises to do if we repent and confess?** (He promises to forgive our sins.)

Whoops, Sploosh! and Pole No More
featuring
LEROY & RUSSELL

Today we are going to learn what *forgiveness* means according to God's Word. Let's start with a story about two brothers whose relationship is in danger.

Leroy couldn't wait to show his younger brother Russell the fishing rod that their grandfather had just given him. It was the same rod that their grandfather had used to teach their father and the boys how to fish. Fishing had been a favorite sport in Leroy's family for years, and Leroy had been waiting for the day he would get his *own* pole. He never expected it would be the one that belonged to his grandfather. Leroy was out in the yard practicing his casting when he saw Russell riding up the street.

"Hey, Russell, look! Grandpa just gave me his fishing pole. Do you want to go down to the lake with me and try it out?"

Russell was envious that Leroy had gotten their grandfather's fishing pole, so he said, "Only if you let me use it first, Big Brother!"

"Wel-l-l, if you're careful. Let's go ask Mom and Dad if we can go!" Leroy said excitedly.

The boys' parents gave them permission to go, so they grabbed a tackle box and headed down the hill to the lake. While Leroy went to catch a few grasshoppers for bait, Russell threw the fishing pole and tackle box into the rowboat. He jumped in, pushed the boat away from the shore, and happily rowed to the middle of the lake.

"I think I can get a better cast if I stand up," he said to himself.

Leroy came back with the bait only to see his little brother standing in the rowboat. "Russell, don't stand up in the boat! And be careful with my new fishing pole!" he yelled from shore.

"No problem, Leroy! I can handle it," said Russell. After his fourth cast, the pole jerked and Russell realized that he'd hooked a fish. As he tried to reel it in, he lost his balance and fell head-first into the lake. When he surfaced he realized that Leroy's pole was gone! The fishing pole had sunk to the bottom of the lake!

"Oh no! I lost the pole!" he cried as he peeked over the rowboat to see an angry Leroy on the shore. "Man, he's really mad! What is he going to do to me?"

- ■ **What choices did Russell make that caused this conflict?**
- ■ **How could Russell take responsibility for his wrong choices?** (Use the 5A's)

If Russell uses the 5A's, one of the things he will say to Leroy is, "Will you please forgive me?" Here are some important facts that Leroy needs to know if he is going to forgive Russell God's way.

Four False Ideas About Forgiveness

People think about forgiveness in many ways. Unfortunately, some of these ways are not consistent with what the Bible says about forgiveness. In order to understand the truth about forgiveness, we first need to recognize these false ideas.

The First False Idea

"You need to FEEL like forgiving before you can really forgive."
When others hurt your feelings, the last thing you feel like doing is forgiving them. In fact, what you often want to do is to hurt them back. Therefore, if forgiveness depended on feelings, it would take a very long time before you forgave people who hurt you.

The Second False Idea

"Forgiveness means FORGETTING about what someone did that hurt you."
When someone wrongs you, it is easy to keep thinking about it for a long time. This is especially true if you were deeply hurt or embarrassed, or if you felt betrayed by a close friend. Therefore, if forgiveness depended on forgetting, you might never forgive some wrongs.

The Third False Idea

"Forgiveness EXCUSES the other person's sin."
Some people think that forgiveness is the same as saying, "It's okay. You didn't do anything wrong." If this were true, you could not honestly forgive people when you know that they really did something wrong.

The Fourth False Idea

"Forgiveness depends on getting a GUARANTEE that someone won't do the same wrong thing again."
When someone wrongs you, you will usually want to find ways to keep from being hurt again. One way to do this is to stay away from those who hurt you until they guarantee they will never do the same wrong thing again. But since everyone is a sinner, none of us can promise that we will not sin again. Therefore, if forgiveness depended on guarantees, there is no way we could really forgive others.

True forgiveness is much better than any of these false ideas. True forgiveness does not depend on feelings, but it does help to change our feelings. It does not depend on forgetting, but it does help us to forget. Forgiveness does not excuse others' wrongs; in fact, saying "I forgive you" is the clearest way of showing that someone did something wrong, but now it is forgiven. And forgiveness does not depend on others' guarantees, but on God's promise to forgive our sins and to help us forgive one another.

Four "I Forgive You" Promises

When people confess their wrongs to us, God wants us to forgive them the same way he forgives us. You can do this by choosing to make four specific promises.

Good Thought

Hurt You Not

Gossip Never

Friends Forever

The Four Promises

God's forgiveness is much different from the false ideas that we just looked at.

- God forgives you *completely*.
- God forgives you *immediately* after you sincerely confess.
- God forgives you *without asking for guarantees* that you will never do the same thing again.

The Bible says we must "be kind and compassionate to one another, forgiving each other, *just as in Christ God forgave you*" (Eph. 4:32; emphasis added).

■ **What do you think it means to forgive just as Christ forgave you?** (Answers will vary.)

God's forgiveness can *never* be earned. Our sin deserves justice and punishment, but God chooses to give forgiveness to those who sincerely confess their sins (review 1 John 1:9). The Lord wants you to forgive others in the same way he forgives you. This means you must choose to give the gift of forgiveness to others. **Forgiveness is a choice** to make four promises to people who hurt or offend you.

The First Promise

I promise I will think good thoughts about you and do good for you.

Good Thought

This is a very important promise, because what you think affects how you feel about people. Thinking good thoughts, especially about people who have hurt you, can help build bridges instead of walls in your relationships—and that glorifies the Lord! God tells you specifically what he wants you to think about other people. In the middle of a Bible passage about a conflict, it says:

"Whatever is true, whatever is noble, whatever is right, whatever is pure, whatever is lovely, whatever is admirable—if anything is excellent or praiseworthy—think about such things" (Phil. 4:8).

The Lord doesn't want you to stop there. He wants you to go the next step and do good for that person.

"But I tell you who hear me: Love your enemies, do good to those who hate you, bless those who curse you, pray for those who mistreat you" (Luke 6:27).

When God helps you to love, do good to, bless and pray for those who have been mean to you, you will usually have better feelings about them eventually. One way to do this is by speaking well about and to the person who hurt you. You can also begin to think of things to do that would help the person—and then do them! That is real evidence of forgiveness.

The Second Promise

I promise I will not bring up this situation to use against you.

Do you ever remind others about what they have done to hurt you? Do others ever remind you about your bad choices? This is the opposite of forgiveness. When God forgives you, he promises never to bring up your sin to use against you. In other words, you won't hear about those sinful attitudes and actions from God again.

"Love . . . keeps no record of wrongs" (1 Cor. 13:5).

The Third Promise

I promise I will not talk to others about what you did.

If you are like most people, you will be tempted to tell other people about what someone has done to hurt you. You may want people to feel sorry for you and side with you instead of with the person who mistreated you. This, too, is the opposite of forgiveness. Gossip usually fuels a conflict and causes more problems between you and others. God teaches us that . . .

"Without gossip a quarrel dies down" (Prov. 26:20).

If you are having a hard time dealing with a problem, it is appropriate to ask someone you trust to help you. In that case, you will need to explain the facts and express your feelings about the conflict. This should not be done to gossip, but to get help to solve the problem and save your friendship.

The Fourth Promise

I promise I will be friends with you again.

This is real evidence of your forgiving attitude toward the person who has asked for forgiveness. This promise means that you will treat the person who hurt you with respect, kindness, and courtesy. It means that you will treat others the way you want God to treat you when you have asked for his forgiveness. It means that when you pray the Lord's Prayer, you can honestly say:

"Forgive me my sins, as I have forgiven those who have sinned against me" (Matt. 6:12, paraphrased).

When you forgive in this way, you are forgiving as the Lord forgives you! Remember that **forgiveness is a choice** to make these four promises no matter how you feel. Whenever you forgive those who have hurt you, you will show God how much you appreciate his gift of forgiveness to you. And that *always* pleases him!

Seeking and Giving Forgiveness

Seeking Forgiveness

When you ask for forgiveness for something you have done, whether it was a sinful choice, an accident, or a careless mistake, you are asking the person you hurt to make the four promises of forgiveness. You want to have the same kind of relationship with the person as you had before the offense. Your confession and the seeking of forgiveness speeds up the healing in your own heart as well as in your relationship with the person you hurt. Without forgiveness, complete healing is impossible. It is also necessary for you to ask for forgiveness from God, because when you sin against people, you also sin against him.

Giving Forgiveness

If you are going to forgive in the same way that the Lord forgives you, you must choose to make the four promises of forgiveness to the person who hurt or offended you. However, if someone has a habit of doing something that hurts or offends you, you may need to seek advice from someone you trust so you can help the hurtful person understand how his choices are affecting you and others. When you remind a person of his sinful habits, it must be for the purpose of trying to solve the problem between the two of you as well as help the person change a sinful habit—not to punish the person with frequent reminders of his sinful choices.

Forgiveness Doesn't Always Cancel Consequences

Even though you are forgiven, you still need to accept the consequences of your choices. If Leroy forgives Russell for losing the fishing pole, Russell should still repair the damage he has caused. Russell could never replace the pole he lost in the lake, but he could buy Leroy a new pole that is similar to the one that he lost. If Russell accepts his responsibility for his carelessness, it will make it easier for Leroy to forgive him.

■ **Think of a time when you were forgiven for something you did. Can you briefly tell us about it?** (Teachers, allow two or three student to share their stories. Try to help them to keep the stories *brief*.)

■ **How did you feel after you were forgiven?**

■ **How do you think others feel after you forgive them?**

When to Forgive

Now let's talk about when you should forgive someone. When people sin against each other, they need to go and be reconciled, which usually means to seek forgiveness and give forgiveness.

When someone's choices are a little hurtful to you, but not really that bad, you may choose to overlook the offense and forgive him in your heart even if he doesn't confess his wrongs. Remember, **forgiveness is a choice**. At a time like this you may choose to think:

"Andy usually doesn't say mean things. He must be having a bad day. I'm just going to forgive him and not make a big deal out of it."

Sometimes people will do things that are very hurtful. If they come to you and use the 5A's in a genuine way, expressing sorrow for their sin and for the effect it had on you, it is important for you to make the four promises of forgiveness. Then you will be forgiving others as the Lord forgave you.

Most people have a difficult time admitting they have done something wrong. They may refuse to confess that they have sinned against you. When this happens, you should still make the first promise of forgiveness, which is to think good thoughts about, and do good to, the person. The other three promises of forgiveness may need to be postponed until the person genuinely confesses and repents of his sin. For instance, if someone's sin against you is serious, you may need to talk to the person about it more than once. If the person still refuses to accept responsibility for his or her sin, you should talk to a parent, relative, teacher, counselor, pastor, or friend who could help you respond to the problem in a way that glorifies God.

When you need to forgive someone, keep in mind that since the Lord is merciful and forgiving toward you, you need to be that way toward others. *God does not say* . . ."I forgive you, but I don't want to have anything to do with you again." Instead, God's forgiveness washes your sins away so that you can be close to him again. With his help, you can strive to forgive others in the same way.

121

How to Forgive

There is a right and a wrong way to express forgiveness toward others. Once someone asks you for forgiveness, the *wrong way* to communicate your forgiveness is by saying, "*That's okay.*" This response says that the person's choice to sin was "okay." But the Bible says it is never okay to sin.

There is a better and more biblical response to the question, "Will you forgive me?" The *right way* to express forgiveness is to say, "*I forgive you.*" When you say these three words, you are making the four promises of forgiveness to the person who hurt you. You are forgiving others just as the Lord forgives you.

Before you forgive someone, you may need to express how you feel about what the person has done. The Apostle Paul says to speak the truth in love (Eph. 4:15). Gently explain how you were affected by the person's choice, express your thanks for his confession, and then say, "*I forgive you.*"

For example, assume Russell genuinely confessed his wrong-doing to Leroy by saying something like this:

"*I admit* I was envious that you got Grandpa's fishing pole. I was careless with it when I took it out in the boat by myself and lost it. *I am so sorry* that it's gone. I'm sure you must be mad at me. I know that another pole can't take the place of the one that belonged to

Grandpa, but *I would like to buy you a new pole* to replace the one I lost. Leroy, *will you please forgive me? Next time* I will be more careful with your things."

Then Leroy could respond by saying something like this:

"Even though I feel bad that Grandpa's fishing pole is lost, I know that you didn't mean to lose it. I'm glad that you honestly admitted what happened. I want you to know that *I forgive you*, Russell. (Leroy could also tell Russell about the four promises of forgiveness.)

Leroy has granted Russell forgiveness. *Granting forgiveness is an event.* When you say the words, "I forgive you," you are making the four promises of forgiveness to the person who hurt or offended you.

Carrying out forgiveness is a process that can take time and prayer. Leroy may have to work at following through on the four promises of forgiveness, because he may be tempted to think bad thoughts about Russell, to remind him of what he did wrong, to gossip about what happened, or to hold him at a distance.

You, too, may struggle with carrying out forgiveness at times. Ask the Lord to help you resist the temptation to be unforgiving and help you forgive others in the same way that Jesus has forgiven you.

FORGIVENESS IS A CHOICE.

Why Forgive?

■ **Why should we forgive other people?** (Answers will vary.)

Forgiveness is not easy. When other people hurt us, our natural tendency is to feel bitter and not want to be around them any more. Jesus knew that we would sometimes struggle with these feelings. So he told a story to help us choose to forgive others even when we don't feel like it (see Matt. 18:21-35).

That story is about a servant who owed the king millions and millions of dollars. He could not pay on time, so the king threatened to throw him in prison. When the servant begged for more time to pay the debt, the king chose to show great mercy: he forgave the debt entirely so the servant would not have to pay back any of it.

As the servant was leaving the king's palace, he met another servant who owed him a few hundred dollars. He demanded that the debt be paid immediately. Even though the other servant begged for time to pay the money, the first servant showed him no mercy. Instead, he had the man thrown in prison until he could pay.

When the king found out what happened, he called the unmerciful servant back to the throne room. "You wicked servant," the king said. "I canceled all that debt of yours because you begged me to! Shouldn't you have had mercy on your fellow servant just as I had on you?" In anger, the king turned him over to the jailers to suffer until he paid back all he owed.

Through this parable Jesus is telling us two important things. First, he is reminding us how much he has forgiven us. The debt created by our sins was so great that Jesus himself had to come and die on the cross to pay it. Jesus wants us to remember that another person's sins against us are very small compared to our sins against God (like comparing a hundred dollars to millions of dollars). When we think of God's wonderful promise of forgiveness and all that Jesus did to earn it for us, we should be willing to forgive others for the things they do wrong.

The second thing Jesus teaches in this parable is that if we choose not to forgive others when they have confessed their wrongs, we will experience painful consequences. When we refuse to forgive, we are sinning against God, and he promises to discipline us (see Heb. 12:5-6). As bitterness grows in our hearts, we will feel miserable and far from God. If we continue to be unforgiving, we may lose precious friendships. And we may find that other people are slow to forgive our sins. When we think about these things, we can see that it is very foolish not to forgive others.

When we are wise and choose to forgive others, we can experience many wonderful consequences. We can know that we are glorifying God by obeying him and imitating his forgiveness. We can find joy in serving others; our forgiveness helps to take away the burden of their guilt and gives them another chance to make good choices in the future. And we can become more like Jesus as we learn to forgive others the same way he has forgiven us.

Wrapping It Up

You have learned a lot about forgiveness in this lesson. You discovered that forgiveness does not depend on feelings, forgetting, or guarantees that someone will never sin against you again. You learned that **forgiveness is a choice** to make "four promises"; when you say, "I forgive you," you are making those four promises to the person who sinned against you.

You also learned that forgiveness is necessary because God has forgiven you so much. Forgiveness is not an option for a Christian—it is a command. Without forgiveness a conflict will never be completely resolved. You need to ask the Lord to help you obey his command to go and be reconciled by seeking forgiveness as well as by forgiving others in the same way God has forgiven you.

Closing Prayer

Dear Lord, thank you for the loving way you forgive me when I sin and make bad choices. Because of what Jesus did for me on the cross, you never hold my sin against me. But I often let my pride keep me from seeking and giving forgiveness. Please help me to remember the high price Jesus had to pay for my forgiveness. Help me to be more forgiving toward others out of love for you; help me to put into practice the four promises of forgiveness; and help me to ask for forgiveness when I have sinned. In Jesus' name,

Amen.

Making It Real

Assign one or more of the suggested activities for Lesson Eight that are found in the Activities and Personal Application section of this lesson. Some of the activities are included in Student Activity Book #8.

Activities and Personal Application

Activity one can be found in Student Activity Book (SAB) #8.

1. Dump the Junk (see SAB 8-10): Sort out the ideas about forgiveness. If an idea is wrong, cross it out and draw a line to the garbage can to show where it belongs. If an idea is good, circle it to show that you want to think that way about forgiveness. (Answers: 1, 3, 4, 8, 9, 11, 13, 14 are wrong ideas; the rest are right)

2. **Seeking forgiveness:**
Tammy and Lynn are playing Monopoly. Tammy disagrees with Lynn about the rules of the game, and finally the girls get into an argument. Tammy gets so upset that she rips up some of the game cards. She stomps out of Lynn's house saying, "I'm never going to play this dumb game with you again!" When Tammy gets home, she goes right to her room and pulls out her Monopoly game. She reads the rules, and to her surprise, discovers that Lynn was right about how to play the game.

Pretend that you are Tammy and write down what you could say to Lynn to resolve this conflict.

Read what you have written. Is your confession complete? Is it sincere? After hearing your confession, would Lynn find it easy or hard to forgive you? Why?

Giving forgiveness:

Now pretend that you are Lynn. Tammy has just used the 5A's to confess that she knows that she was wrong about the rules, wrong to argue with you, and wrong to rip up the game cards. She says that she will buy a new Monopoly game to replace the one she ruined.

Write down what you could say to Tammy to reassure her of your forgiveness. Think about how to include the four promises of forgiveness. How could you show Tammy that you are serious about forgiving her?

Read what you have written. Would Tammy be assured of your forgiveness?

3. Think of someone you have had a hard time forgiving (and who know there is a problem between you). You may still be angry with him, or you may be ignoring him and not speaking to him.

Write down what you need to say and do to really forgive him. (Maybe you need first to use the 5A's to confess that you have been wrong not to forgive him.)

Go to him during this coming week to let him know that you forgive him. Record his response. Could you have done something more to help him know that you really forgive him?

Dig into the Word

Memory Verse:

Ephesians 4:32

Other Relevant Bible Verses:

Psalm 130:3-4   Mark 11:25
Matthew 18:21-35   Colossians 3:13
Luke 17:3-4

Applicable Bible Stories:

Assign one or more of the following passages to help children analyze conflict situations in the Bible.

The stoning of Stephen (Acts 7:54-60)

The prodigal son (Luke 15:11-32)

Jesus' crucifixion (Luke 23:26-34)

The Lesson Summary

Bible Memory Verse

"Be kind and compassionate to one another, forgiving one another, just as in Christ God forgave you" (Eph. 4:32).

Key Principle

Forgiveness is a choice.

The Main Points of This Lesson

1. Forgiveness is not . . .

Four false ideas about forgiveness:
- People need to *feel* like forgiving someone before they can really forgive.
- Forgiveness means *forgetting* about what someone did that hurt you.
- Forgiveness *excuses* a person's sin.
- Forgiveness depends on getting a guarantee that someone won't do the same wrong thing again.

2. Forgiveness is . . .

God's forgiveness is much different.
- God forgives you *completely*.
- God forgives you *immediately* after a sincere confession.
- God forgives you *without asking for guarantees* that you will never do the same wrong thing again.

The *four promises* of forgiveness are:
- I promise I will *think good thoughts about you* and do good for you.
- I promise I will not *bring up this situation to use against you*.
- I promise I will not *talk to others* about what you did.
- I promise I will *be friends with you again*.

3. Seeking and giving forgiveness

When you seek forgiveness, you are asking the person you sinned against to grant you the four promises of forgiveness.
If you are going to forgive someone else, you must choose to give the four promises of forgiveness to the one who hurt or offended you.
Forgiveness does not cancel consequences.

4. When to forgive?

Full forgiveness is granted after there has been *repentance and confession*.

5. How to express forgiveness?

The *wrong response* to the question, "Will you forgive me?" is "*That's okay*."
The *right response* to the question, "Will you forgive me?" is "*I forgive you*."
Granting forgiveness is an *event*. Carrying out forgiveness is a *process* that can take time.

6. Why forgive?

The reason we should forgive others is because *God has forgiven us*.

Part Three

Preventing Conflict

If your students are going to reduce conflict in their lives, they will need to depend on God to change their hearts and help them to alter their choices. They also need to learn how to identify what they said or did that contributed to a conflict and what they can do to change in the future. When your students are in the heat of conflict, it is typical for them to talk to everyone else about the problem instead of going directly to the person with whom they are having a conflict. When they do communicate their thoughts and concerns to the other person, they often do it in a way that stirs up anger instead of resolving the conflict.

Your students need to understand that what they say and how they say it will have a great effect on how people listen and respond to them. If they choose to communicate respectfully, it is likely that they will be able to resolve, and even prevent, conflict. The opposite is also true: if they speak or act disrespectfully, they shouldn't be surprised when others become angry with them and conflict clouds their relationships. In this section you will be teaching your students how to evaluate and alter what they say and do, and how to go to someone in private to discuss problems and concerns effectively.

Altering Choices

> Those who **plan what is good** find love and faithful-ness.
>
> Proverbs 14:22

Lesson Goal:

To help students discover how to make right choices by thinking before they act.

Lesson Objective:

By God's grace students will learn:
To use the STAY Plan to help them alter their future choices.

Key Principle:

It's never too late to start doing what's right.

Lesson Needs:

Bible
Student Activity Book #9
Worksheet Four—Altering Choices (Appendix C).

Begin with Prayer

Begin the lesson with prayer. Ask the Lord to help your students to learn and apply the STAY Plan. If you have assigned homework, collect or review the assignments.

Review and Setting the Stage

- **How many of you have had an opportunity to use the 5A's this past week?** (Allow a few students to share their stories briefly.)

- **Can anyone name the four promises of forgiveness?** (I promise I will think good thoughts about you and do good for you. I promise I will not bring up this situation to use against you. I promise I will not talk to others about what you did. I promise I will be friends with you again.)

- **Have the four promises helped you in any way? How?** (Accept brief and appropriate answers.)

Good for you! People will know that you are *serious* about peacemaking if you accept responsibility for your choices without arguing or pouting, and if you depend on God to help you to alter your choices and forgive others as the Lord forgave you.

Today we are going to learn about a way that can help you alter your choices.

- **Does anyone know what it means to alter your choices?** (It's turning and going in a different direction—to make different choices.)

IT'S NEVER TOO LATE TO START DOING WHAT'S RIGHT.

Test Cheat, Shredded Sheet

featuring
TONY & MR. CHUNG

Some people feel trapped, thinking that their choices will never change. But they don't have to feel hopeless, because Jesus can help everyone to alter their choices! With him, **it's never too late to start doing what's right.** Listen to a story about a boy who needs to learn to alter his choices.

Tony got into the habit of cheating on homework and tests. Mr. Chung, his teacher, gave him a final warning—the next time he cheated, he would have serious consequences to face. When Mr. Chung assigned a big history exam for Thursday, Tony knew that he really needed to study to get a passing grade this quarter. It was only Monday, and this time he was going to be prepared for the test! Each night, however, Tony found something else to do besides studying. Thursday morning arrived and Tony hadn't even looked at his history book or notes. As he began to panic, a thought flashed through his mind. "Matt just moved next to me. Since he is the class brain and always gets 100's on his tests, I'll copy off his paper and Mr. Chung won't find out that I didn't study." When Tony followed through with his plan, Mr. Chung caught him looking at Matt's answers. Mr. Chung took Tony's paper, tore it up, and gave him a zero for the test.

Tony fooled himself into thinking he could deceive his teacher and no one would know what he did.

■ **What are some of the possible root causes of Tony's choice to cheat?** (Selfishness—he wanted to please himself instead of studying history. Laziness—he didn't want to do the work. Pride—he wanted his teacher and his classmates to think that he was smart. Deceitfulness—he didn't want anyone to know that he hadn't studied.)

Tony now has two choices that he can make:

● Play the blame game, which will make the problem worse.
● Use the 5A's to accept responsibility for his choice and plan how to alter his choice in the future.
■ **What will probably happen if he chooses to play the blame game?**

Role Play Activity: Act out what Tony would do if he played the blame game.

S.T.A.Y. Out of Conflict

We do not have to make the same wrong choices over and over again.
We can STAY out of conflict if we stop and think before we act.

The STAY Plan

It's important to remember that the Lord wants us to make good choices and do what is right. Even if you are in the habit of making bad choices, **it's never too late to start doing what's right.** God is pleased to help you plan how to alter your choices from bad to good. "Those who plan what is good find love and faithfulness" (Prov. 14:22). "Listen, my son, and be wise, and keep your heart on the right path" (Prov. 23:19). The STAY Plan can help you to stay on the right path. STAY stands for Stop-Think-Act-Yea! Let's walk through the STAY Plan to learn how to alter choices.

Stop

The first step in the STAY Plan is to stop what you are doing wrong and think carefully about how to make wiser choices. This process can involve two parts.

Identify the wrong choice you made and the root of it. Be honest with yourself and others about your part in the conflict.

Tony needs to truthfully admit to himself and others that he has a problem with cheating. He also needs to identify the roots of his choice to cheat: selfishness, pride, laziness, and deceitfulness.

Get help so that you can make wise choices next time. You can ask the Lord for help and ask people you trust for advice. Be careful not to ask people who will give you bad advice. Remember, wise advice will always be consistent with God's Word. Tony could pray:

Dear Lord, I confess that I am having trouble with cheating on my assignments and tests. I know that you want me to be honest, and cheating is not honest. Please forgive me for my selfishness, pride, laziness, and deceitfulness. I am asking you for help so that I can make wise and right choices. I am asking you to help me to stop cheating and to do my own work. In Jesus' name, Amen.

Tony could also ask some people he trusts for advice as to how he can stop cheating and start doing his own work.

■ **Can you think of some trustworthy people he could ask for advice?** (Parents, other relatives, teacher, pastor, friend, Sunday school teacher, or a neighbor.)

LAZINESS

Think

Think about and list a variety of possible choices and their predictable consequences for the situation. Include some choices that could get you into more conflict, so that you will see the bad consequences that result from continued bad choices. Let's analyze Tony's choices and their predictable consequences.

Choice One: Choose to study for tests.

Predictable Consequences:

- He would be prepared for tests.
- He could feel confident that he knows the material.
- He could get good grades.
- He would earn respect from others for good work.

Choice Two: Tony could choose to watch TV instead of studying for tests.

Predictable Consequences:

- He won't be prepared for tests.
- He would feel worried and afraid when it was time to take a test.
- He would be tempted to cheat.

Choice Three: Tony could continue to cheat on tests and assignments.

Predictable Consequences:

- He would risk being caught and getting a zero.
- His classmates would not want to sit by him because they also might get zeros.
- He could get a bad reputation for cheating and people wouldn't trust him.

Choice Four: Tony could ask to sit in the study corner to do his work and to take tests.

Predictable Consequences:

- He would not be able to cheat by looking at someone else's work.
- He could get better grades and a better reputation by not cheating.
- Neither he nor his friends would get zeros if he didn't cheat from their work.

Now circle all the good choices and cross out all the bad choices. *Select the best choice* from the circled ones and *plan how to put it into action.* The best option may not be the easiest one, but it will usually resolve the conflict or prevent future ones. It will also please and glorify God.

As you develop your plan, think about *who* is involved, *what* you need to do, *when* and *how* you need to do it, and *where* to carry it out.

Let's say that Tony decides on the first and fourth choices—to study for his tests and to ask to sit in the study corner to do his work and take tests.

Tony's Plan:

- Use the 5A's to confess his problem with cheating to Mr. Chung.
- Pray for God to help him do what is right.
- Turn off the TV and study in the evenings.
- Ask if he can use the study corner during work and test times.
- Listen quietly to Mr. Chung as he gives directions.
- Take all his materials to the study corner.
- Work quietly and independently until he completes the assignment or test.
- Hand in his assignment or test.
- Study more diligently in the future so he won't want to cheat.

Act

Follow through with your plan, praying that God will help you do what is right.

Tony could pray for help to carry out his plan:

Dear Lord, I am powerless to stop cheating, but you are powerful and you are faithful. You live in me, Jesus! Your Word says that "I can do everything through him who gives me strength." Please give me your power to do what is right and follow through with my plan. In Jesus' name, Amen.

Then Tony would begin to follow through with his plan.

Evaluate your plan. Ask yourself: Did my plan work? If it didn't, you can look at the list of other good choices you could make and then develop a new plan.

Yea!

If your plan worked, celebrate and thank the Lord that he helped you alter a bad choice and resolve a problem.

Learning how to alter choices takes time, so don't give up when you feel like it's too hard to change. Instead, use the STAY Plan to alter choices. It can help you think through the problem and how it can be solved. By using this plan, you won't have to feel trapped into thinking that you have no other choice in the matter. You have many possible choices that can solve the problem (at least from your side) and keep you from getting in trouble. At first following the STAY Plan will require time and effort, but eventually you will think through it quickly and come up with a wise solution that would glorify God. Remember, **it's never too late to start doing what's right**.

Wrapping It Up

The STAY Plan can help you take charge of your choices. By using this plan you don't have to be in trouble all the time. God will help you make good choices. When you do, you will please the Lord, and more people will trust and respect you. Good choices are worth it!

Remember that other people may not change their choices, and they may try to keep the conflict going. However, you can do a lot yourself to resolve or prevent conflicts by using the 5A's and the STAY Plan.

The Lord expects you to take responsibility only for your choices. "If it is possible, as far as it depends on you, live at peace with everyone" (Rom. 12:18). May God bless you as you seek his help to alter your choices.

Closing Prayer

Dear Lord, altering my choices takes a lot of work, and I need your power so that I will be able to really change. Please help me to think of creative and good choices to resolve my conflicts with others. Help me to take responsibility for what I do, even if others don't take responsibility for their choices. Thank you for loving me so much that you will change my heart and help me to repent from my sinful choices! In Jesus' name, Amen.

Making It Real

Assign one or more of the suggested activities for Lesson Nine in the Activities and Personal Application section of this lesson. Some of the activities are included in Student Activity Book #9.

Activities and Personal Application

Activities one and two can be found in Student Activity Book (SAB) #9.

1. Help Aaron to Alter His Choices (see SAB 9-9): Using the STAY plan, help Aaron to make a better choice.

2. Word Search (see SAB 9-10): Find the key words on peacemaking in the puzzle.

3. Read the following story. Use the STAY Plan to help Josh alter his bad choice.

Josh and Luke both wanted to play soccer during the noon recess. But as they approached the equipment box, they saw that there was only one soccer ball left. Just as Luke reached for the ball, Josh shoved him away, grabbed the ball, and ran out the door to the playground yelling, "Next time don't get in my way!" Their teacher saw what Josh did and made him come inside and sit through the rest of recess.

Use Worksheet Four (Appendix C) to record your ideas.

4. Pretend that you have had a bad habit of interrupting your parents when they are on the telephone. Using the STAY Plan, think about how to alter your choice. Use Worksheet Four (Appendix C) to record your answers.

5. Use the STAY Plan to alter one of your bad choices. Use Worksheet Four (Appendix C) to record your answers.

Dig into the Word

Memory Verse:

Proverbs 14:22

Other Relevant Bible Verses:

Psalm 20:4
Proverbs 15:22
Proverbs 16:3
Acts 26:20

Applicable Bible Stories:

Assign one or more of the following passages to help students analyze conflict situations in the Bible.

The prodigal son (Luke 15:11-24)

Zacchaeus (Luke 19:1-9)

The Lesson Summary

Bible Memory Verse

"Those who plan what is good find love and faithfulness" (Prov. 14:22).

Key Principle

It's never too late to start doing what's right.

The Main Points of the Lesson

The STAY Plan

> To alter a choice means to *change* a choice from bad to good. Use the STAY Plan to alter choices.
>
> **Stop**: *Identify the choice* and *root cause* that got you into the conflict. *Get help* to know what to do now. *Pray* for wisdom.
>
> **Think**: *Think of many choices* and their *predictable consequences* (both good and bad). *Select the best choice* and *plan* how to put it into action.
>
> **Act**: *Follow through* with your plan. *Evaluate your plan*. Did it work? If not, try again, using another choice.
>
> **Yea!** It worked! *Thank the Lord and celebrate.*

He who **guards his mouth** and his tongue keeps himself from calamity.

Proverbs 21:23

Lesson Goal:

To help students understand that what they say and how they say it can prevent or cause conflict.

Lesson Objectives:

By God's grace students will learn:

1. Why communication is important.
2. The difference between verbal and non-verbal communication.
3. What to communicate.
4. How to communicate effectively.

Key Principle:

Think before you speak.

Lesson Needs:

Bible
Student Activity Book #10
Worksheet Five—Using Respectful Words (Appendix C)

Begin with Prayer

Begin the lesson with prayer that your students will learn to prevent conflict by communicating to others in a respectful way. As you discuss the principles in this lesson, remember to encourage and praise appropriate responses to questions.

Review and Setting the Stage

- **Can you remember what STAY stands for?** (Stop/Think/Act/Yea!)

- **Have any of you used the STAY Plan to alter choices? How?**

- **What kind of choice is it to use the STAY Plan?** (A wise-way choice.)

Today we are going to begin to study another wise-way choice: how to prevent conflict by communicating in a respectful way. What we say and how we say it will have a great effect on how people listen and respond to us. If we choose to communicate respectfully, it is likely that we will be able to resolve or even prevent conflict and stay on top of the slippery slope. We are going to learn interesting and helpful information that can help us communicate more respectfully. You will discover how important it is to **think before you speak**.

Cancelled Canoe Blues

featuring
CARLOS & DAD

NO, STEVE, WE DON'T HAVE ANY IMPORTANT PLANS TODAY.

Listen to a story about a boy who communicated his thoughts and feelings to his family. Be prepared to tell me if you think his communication helped to solve the problem or made it worse.

"It seemed like this day would never come," thought Carlos excitedly, " but it's finally here. I know Dad won't forget this time that he promised to take me canoeing today!"

Carlos was quickly gathering his gear for the trip when the telephone rang. He was shocked to hear his father say, "I'd be happy to come to the office this morning, Mr. Perez. I don't have any plans for the weekend anyway. We'll get that project done on time yet!"

Anger and disappointment grew inside of Carlos as he overheard his father's phone conversation with his boss. How could his dad have forgotten that he had promised to take Carlos canoeing today? This was the third time this summer that his father had broken his promise to take him out in their new canoe.

Carlos had a habit of holding his thoughts and feelings inside, so it was hard for his family to understand him at times. This morning was no different. At the breakfast table, Carlos pouted and refused to talk to anyone. When his father asked Carlos if there was something bothering him, he snarled, "No! Besides, you wouldn't care if there was!" With that, Carlos stomped out of the kitchen and slammed the door behind him.

His dad followed immediately and told him to go to his room for being so disrespectful.

"So much for a fun day canoeing. I should have known he wouldn't remember our plans," Carlos grumbled as he flopped down on his bed.

The Bible says, "A gentle answer turns away wrath, but a harsh word stirs up anger" (Prov. 15:1).

■ **Did Carlos' way of communicating his thoughts and feelings to his father prevent or stir up conflict? Did he solve the problem or make it worse?** (The way Carlos chose to communicate made the problem worse.)

That's right. Carlos communicated his thoughts and feelings to his father in a way that got him into trouble. Instead of being heard and understood, he was sent to his room.

Has something like this ever happened to you? If it has, then you, like Carlos, need to learn a better way to communicate so that others will be more likely to listen to you and understand you. You need to learn to **think before you speak.** Let's talk about the why, what, and how of effective communication that pleases Jesus.

141

Think Before You Speak

You will often get into conflict if you don't think before you speak. If your brain is asleep while your mouth is working, you will often send messages that cause problems for you and others.

Words We Speak

Body Language

Sending Messages

- **What do you think it means to communicate?** (Answers will vary.)

Here is a simple definition that we will use for the word *communicate: to send and receive messages.*

- **Why is communication important?** (Answers will vary.)

One of the main purposes of communication is to help others understand you better and you to understand them. The more clearly and respectfully you communicate, the more likely it will be that others will understand and respond appropriately to your thoughts, feelings, needs and desires. Good communication does not guarantee that you will get your own way, but it can increase understanding and prevent unnecessary conflict.

Another purpose of communication is to build others up. God wants the words you speak to be helpful, encouraging, and good for the listener to hear. He is never pleased when you make fun of someone, talk back, or use words that intentionally hurt another person. The Apostle Paul says: "Do not let any unwholesome talk come out of your mouths, but only what is helpful for building others up according to their needs, that it may benefit those who listen" (Eph. 4:29). People will usually respond favorably to you when your communication is helpful. Sometimes you will communicate to:

- Encourage or praise others.
- Express your thoughts and feelings.
- Help someone recognize his or her sin.
- Ask questions so you can understand another person's viewpoint.
- Share something that the Lord has been teaching you through his Word.

This kind of communication is helpful and constructive.

On the other hand, communication that tears others down will usually cause conflict. For instance, your communication may:

- Ridicule someone.
- Express anger at someone when you don't get your own way.
- Spread rumors about another person.
- Carelessly hurt a person's feelings.

This kind of communication is hurtful and destructive.

Once you decide *why* you need to communicate with someone, then it will be necessary to think about *what* you want to communicate and *how* to do so in the best way possible. In other words, you need to **think before you speak**.

Good facial expression

"I messages"

I WAS WRONG, DAD, TO BE DISRESPECTFUL TO YOU. I APOLOGIZE. WILL YOU PLEASE FORGIVE ME?

Respectful tone of voice

Verbal and Nonverbal

Before you communicate, you need to think about the verbal and nonverbal messages you are going to send to other people. *Verbal communication* means that you send messages using words, sounds, or tone of voice. This is done by:

- Talking
- Whispering
- Shouting
- Mumbling
- Screaming
- Talking back
- Sighing
- (Teachers, ask students for other examples.)

Verbal communication is usually easier to understand than nonverbal communication, because words have certain meanings. You can understand what I mean if I say:

- "Hi!"
- "I'll be home at 4 o'clock this afternoon."
- "Please clean up the mess in the kitchen."

Nonverbal communication means that you send messages by your actions, gestures, or facial expressions. This is sometimes called body language.

- Eye contact
- Facial expressions
- Body posture
- Listening

See if you can tell me what I am communicating with these nonverbal messages. (Teachers, act out the following messages.)

- Wave "hello" to a friend.
- Slam the door and look angry.
- Slump your shoulders and look sad.
- Jump up and down and act excited.
- Motion with your arm to come here.
- Roll your eyes to look disgusted or bored.

Teaching Tip

Nonverbal communication will be discussed in more detail in the next lesson.

"I Messages"

When you communicate verbally, it is important to **think before you speak** and plan to put words together in a respectful and responsible way. One way to do this is to use "I messages." These messages begin with the word "I" instead of "you." Rather than focusing on what others have done wrong, "I messages" describe your situation, feelings, or thoughts and show that you are taking responsibility for your part in a conflict. The 5A's are "I messages" to use when you need to confess sinful attitudes and actions. But there are other uses for "I messages." For example, you can use "I messages" to:

- Demonstrate that you are *taking responsibility* for your thoughts, beliefs, feelings, needs and desires, and *explain* your reasons for them.
- *Confront a person* about something he or she has done.
- *Request* that a need be met or a desire be considered.
- *Ask* for something you want.

- *Express* thanks and appreciation.

Let's think about Carlos for a moment. If he had used "I messages" to express his feelings and respectfully confront his father, he could have helped to prevent the conflict that occurred between them. He could have said something like:

"Dad, I am disappointed, because I thought you said we were going canoeing this morning."

By using these words, Carlos could communicate his feelings to his father in a loving way. The "I message" doesn't blame or accuse Carlos' father, but helps him to understand how his son feels about a broken promise. Carlos is not responsible for how his father responds to this confrontation. In fact, his father may respond by slipping into the escape or attack zone. Even so, Carlos is only responsible for how he communicates his thoughts and feelings to his father. It is important for him to **think before he speaks** so he won't provoke a worse conflict.

What to Communicate

Like Carlos, you need to **think before you speak.** Think about using "I messages," which will communicate to others that you are taking responsibility for your sinful attitudes and actions, as well as your thoughts and feelings about what others have done. "I messages" should not be used to manipulate others to satisfy your desires. Instead, they should be spoken to improve understanding, benefit the listener, and build stronger relationships. How well people listen to you is partly up to you and your choice to communicate respectfully. You will choose to communicate many things, such as:

- What you think
- What you see
- What you believe
- Questions you have
- How you feel
- Experiences you have had
- What you need
- Thanks and appreciation
- What you want
- Confession and Confrontation

■ **Can you think of other things that you communicate?** (Accept appropriate answers.)

You will send these messages by using verbal communication (with words or sounds) or nonverbal communication (without words or sounds). The way you communicate verbally and nonverbally is a choice. Like other choices, what you say and how you say it can lead to conflict. When you choose to send messages by glaring, arguing, throwing temper tantrums, or pouting, you will usually slide down the slippery slope and get into fights and quarrels with others.

We need to communicate to let people know what is going on in our minds and hearts. Clear and careful communication can help people understand us. Look at the following examples of clear or confusing communication that can either reduce the risk of conflict or create misunderstandings and relationship problems. Notice the use of "I messages."

Identify Facts: Facts are things that exist or occur. For example:

"Hey! You need to pick me up at seven o'clock. Be there!" (Disrespectful)

"The game begins at 7:30 tonight. If I'm late again, the coach says I'm off the team. Could you please pick me up at seven o'clock?" (Respectful)

Explain Thoughts: Thoughts include ideas, opinions, attitudes, beliefs, and evaluations. For example:

"Math is dumb!" (Disrespectful)

"I am not doing as well in math as I thought I would." (Respectful)

Express Feelings: Explain how people and circumstances affect you. For example:

"Bobby makes me sick." (Disrespectful)

Teaching Tip

Alternate the order in which you read the examples in this section. Ask your students to identify which are respectful or disrespectful communication.

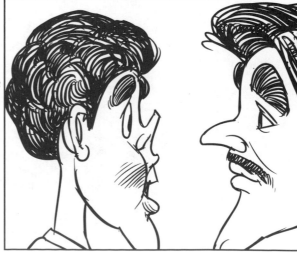

146

"I feel angry when Bobby makes fun of me." (Respectful)

Discuss Plans: Describe plans you have made and seek permission to carry them out. For example:

"I am going to Lisa's house. I don't know when I'll be back." (Disrespectful)

"I'd like to go to Lisa's house. We want to plan a surprise party for Molly's birthday. Would that be okay with you, Mom?" (Respectful)

Describe Your Needs or Desires: Needs are things you need in order to live, while desires include things you want. For example:

"Get me a new bike!" (Disrespectful)

"Dad, I'd sure like to have a new bike. The one I've got is just too small for me this year." (Respectful)

Express Thanks and Appreciation: Always express thanks for what others have done. Ingratitude is at the root of many conflicts and relationship problems. For example:

"It's about time you made something for dinner that I like." (Disrespectful)

"I sure liked the pizza you made for dinner, Mom. Thanks for letting me choose the menu tonight!" (Respectful)

Confront a Person

At times you may need to talk to other people about something they did that was wrong or hurtful. This is called *confrontation*. It is often wise to ask them to give you permission to explain how their choices affected you or someone else. Be careful that you don't use the word "you" to start your confrontation. "You" is an accusatory word. It usually makes people respond by arguing and excusing their behavior. A respectful "I message" can help people understand how their choices affected you, but it doesn't demand a response from them. Many people will listen to a respectful confrontation and respond

with an apology. No matter how they respond, you are only responsible for how you communicate! Listen to the following examples and tell me which one is respectful and responsible.

"You never spend time with me." (Disrespectful)

"Dad, may I explain to you how your choices affected me? I felt so disappointed when you broke your promise to take me canoeing on Saturday. It's happened before, and it's hard for me to believe you when you say you are going to do something." (Respectful)

■ **Can you think of other examples of respectful confrontations?**

Any communication can lead to conflict if you do not **think before you speak**. But if you communicate thoughtfully and respectfully, your words can build bridges between you and other people. They will understand you better, and they will usually respond to you in a more respectful way.

> **Role Play Activity:** You need to confront your friend. He asked you to go swimming with him on Saturday morning. He said he would come for you at 10 o'clock, but he didn't show up. Later, you found out that he took another friend to the pool with him. Think about what you are going to say and how you are going to say it so you don't make the problem worse.

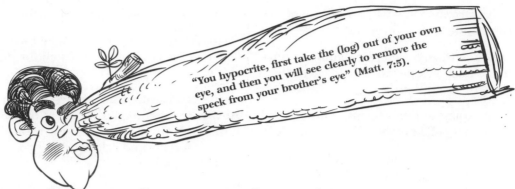

"You hypocrite, first take the (log) out of your own eye, and then you will see clearly to remove the speck from your brother's eye" (Matt. 7:5).

Confess Before Confronting

There may be times when you sense tension between you and another peron. You've tried to overlook the times you've been hurt, but there seems to be a growing problem between the two of you. If you slip into the escape zone, you will probably do nothing except become more angry and resentful toward the person. If instead you slide into the attack zone, you will probably try to retaliate by saying or doing things that hurt the other person. Neither of these responses will please and glorify the Lord, nor will they keep you on top of the slippery slope. You have another choice.

First, you need to examine your own choices and use the 5A's to confess your responsibility for any part you played in the conflict. There are three reasons for this:

- First, you need to take responsibility for your part because God tells you to do so (see Matt. 7:5).

- Second, your confession will prevent the other person from using your sin as an excuse for his or her sins.

- Finally, your confession will be a good example for others to follow. Your confession could make it easier for the other person to confess as well.

After using the 5A's, you can confront the other person about the things that he or she did that hurt or troubled you. By using "I messages," you can explain to the person how his or her choices affected you. It is important to remember that confrontation must always be done respectfully if it is to glorify God and benefit the other person. It should never be done to hurt someone or just to dump your feelings on someone else.

Role Play Activity: You have made friends with a new girl in your neighborhood who just moved to this country from Viet Nam. Two of your other neighborhood friends ridicule her because her skin color is different from theirs. And they have started ignoring you because you are her friend. At first you give them dirty looks and talk about them behind their backs. But then you decide that you need to respectfully confront your friends about how their choices are affecting you and your new friend. Your friends claim to be Christians. Remember to use the 5A's to confess your contribution to the conflict first.

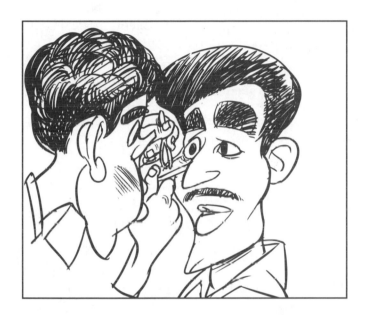

Overlook or Confront?

When you are deciding whether or not to confront a person about a problem, it is always a good idea to remember Proverbs 19:11, where God gives wise advice: "A man's wisdom gives him patience; it is to his glory to overlook an offense."

In other words, it is wise and pleases God when you overlook or ignore most of the "nit-picky" things others do that bother you. (For example, if your brother ate the last bowl of your favorite cereal for breakfast, it is probably not something that is worth confronting him about.)

But if someone has a sinful habit or if you find yourself getting more upset about a situation, as Carlos did, it is better to confront the person about the problem in a respectful way.

■ **Do you think it would be wise for Carlos to respectfully confront his father about breaking his commitment to go canoeing?** (Yes. This has become a pattern that is seriously affecting their relationship.)

149

Needs, Desires, or Demands?

Let's talk about needs and desires for a moment. There are many needs that are legitimate needs, but when they are communicated in a sinful way, they become demands and can lead to conflict. For instance, you may really need a new pair of shoes. But if you throw a temper tantrum because your mother can't get them for you today, you have turned a need into a selfish desire. You need to confess that you gave in to your sinful heart instead of waiting patiently for things you need or want. Remember, "He who conceals his sins does not prosper, but whoever confesses and renounces them finds mercy" (Prov. 28:13).

You can have a need or desire for something without making it a demand. You can communicate your desire in a respectful way, and then respond just as respectfully if you don't get what you want. For example, you may have a desire to have a friend spend the night at your house, but your parents may say no because they want to have a quiet evening at home with just the family. You can respectfully accept what they say without arguing or pouting, even though you really want your friend to sleep over.

It is important to remember that not all desires are wrong or bad. It is when you turn your desires into demands that problems arise. If your parents say that you cannot have a friend over and you respond with a temper tantrum, then you have turned your desire into a demand. That is a sinful response to a legitimate, non-sinful desire.

Role Play Activity: A new friend has asked you to go to the mall on Saturday afternoon to "hang out." When you ask for permission to go, your parents say, "No, you may not go." Act out both a wrong way and a right way for you to respond to this situation.

150

Effective Communication

We have discovered that we communicate both verbally and nonverbally. We have discussed the importance of using "I messages" to effectively communicate thoughts, feelings, needs, desires, and confrontations. It is also important to know that we will choose to send verbal and nonverbal messages in two other ways: disrespectfully, which is sinful and often causes conflict, or respectfully, which is good and glorifies the Lord.

Respectful or Disrespectful Talk

Disrespectful communication sends messages that you are demanding your own way and will accept nothing less. It is likely that you will have unpleasant consequences for choosing to communicate in this selfish and sinful way. In addition, it's possible that people won't listen to you or even consider what you are saying when you communicate in this manner.

■ **What are some examples of disrespectful communication?** (To grumble, complain, criticize, ridicule, curse, gossip, talk back, nag, whine, pout, argue, or throw temper tantrums.)

The opposite is also true. If you **think before you speak** and choose to communicate respectfully, you will send messages with your words and your tone of voice that most people will listen to. You will communicate to build up (being helpful), not to tear down (being hurtful). When you communicate respectfully, people will probably consider what you have to say. They may not always agree with you, and they may not let you have what you want, but they will be more likely to listen to your respectful communication without getting angry.

■ **What are some examples of respectful and responsible communication?** ("I messages" that communicate confession, confrontation, thanks and appreciation, thoughts, feelings, needs, desires.)

Respectful communication is obedient to God. It is his desire that children respect persons in authority, especially their parents. God clearly communicates this desire in the commandment given to Moses at Mount Sinai: "Honor your father and your mother, so that you may live long in the land the Lord your God is giving you" (Ex. 20:12). The Lord echoes this desire in the New Testament through the Apostle Paul: "Children, obey your parents in the Lord, for this is right. 'Honor your father and mother'—which is the first commandment with a promise—'that it may go well with you and that you may enjoy long life on the earth'" (Eph. 6:1-3). Even though there are many reasons why you should communicate respectfully, the most important reason is because God tells us to.

The Bible says, "He who guards his mouth and his tongue keeps himself from calamity" (Prov. 21:23). This verse teaches that you need to think about what you say and how you say it so you don't make a problem worse. Ask God to give you a righteous heart and a respectful mouth. Always remember to speak to others as you want them to speak to you. Doing so pleases the Lord and builds stronger relationships.

THINK BEFORE YOU SPEAK.

151

Wrapping It Up

In this lesson we learned that we need to **think before we speak**. We need to think about why we need to communicate; what we need to communicate; and how we can communicate more effectively. We also discovered that we will send verbal and nonverbal messages to others in a respectful or disrespectful way. If we are going to communicate to others in a way that pleases the Lord, then we must choose to communicate respectfully. When we send messages in a respectful way it is more likely that we will be heard and understood.

We will stop here for today. During the upcoming week, I want you to pay close attention to the kind of words you use to communicate.

Do you communicate to others in a respectful way? In the next lesson, we will talk about using respectful communication as a way to resolve or prevent conflict. With God's help, you can learn to "guard your mouth and your tongue and keep yourself from calamity."

Closing Prayer

Dear Lord, I know that many conflicts I get into happen because I communicate in a sinful way. I say and do things that are disrespectful and then I wonder why people get upset with me. Please forgive me for communicating from my selfish heart. Help me to learn to communicate my thoughts, my feelings, my needs, and my desires in a respectful way. Help me to think about what I say and how I say it. Please help me to prevent conflict by communicating in a way that pleases you. In Jesus' name,
Amen.

Making It Real

Assign one or more of the suggested activities for Lesson Ten that are found in the Activities and Personal Application section of this lesson. Some of the activities are included in Student Activity Book #10.

Activities and Personal Application

Activities one, two, and three can be found in Student Activity Book (SAB) #10.

1. Brain Benders (see SAB 10-9): Follow the instructions to learn how important it is to think before you speak.

2. Run Them Through the Washer (see SAB 10-10): Run the reckless words through a "washing machine" and write different words that would help and encourage the person to whom you are talking.

3. Watch a television show or video and write down examples of disrespectful communication that you hear. With a parent, discuss how you could change the disrespectful examples to respectful communication.

4. Choose a partner. Using nonverbal communication (sending messages without words or sounds), you will need to give your partner directions to:

- Put a puzzle together
- Know where to get a drink of water
- Find a certain book on the bookshelf
- Draw a picture of a bicycle
- Get an apple and peel it

5. Play a game of Charades. Think of something that you want to communicate and then, without using words, act it out in front of the group or class. They will have one minute to guess what you are trying to communicate. (Teachers, it would be helpful if you prepared a list of people, places, or things that your students could act out during this game. Write the ideas on individual 3x5 cards. Have each student choose a card and act out a charade to try to get the other students to guess what was written on his or her card.)

Dig into the Word

Memory Verse:

Proverbs 21:23

Other Relevant Bible Verses:

Proverbs 10:19
Proverbs 12:18
Proverbs 15:1
Proverbs 21:23
Matthew 15:18-19
Ephesians 4:29
James 1:19

Applicable Bible Stories:

Assign one or more of the following passages to help students analyze conflict situations in the Bible.

David, Nabal and Abigail
(1 Sam. 25:1-35)
Nathan confronting David
(2 Sam. 12:1-13)

The Lesson Summary

Bible Memory Verse

"He who guards his mouth and his tongue keeps himself from calamity" (Prov. 21:23).

Key Principle

Think before you speak.

The Main Points of This Lesson

1. Sending messages is important.

We *communicate* when we send or receive messages.
One of the main purposes of communication is to *help others understand you better* and *you to understand them.*
Another purpose for communication is to *build others up.*

2. Verbal and nonverbal communication

Verbal communication means that you use words, tone of voice, or sounds to send messages.
A respectful way to communicate your thoughts, feelings, needs and desires is by using "*I messages.*"
Nonverbal communication means that you send messages using actions, gestures, or facial expressions.
Examples of *nonverbal communication*:

- Eye contact
- Body posture
- Facial expressions
- Gestures

3. What to communicate:

- What we think
- What we believe
- How we feel
- What we need
- What we want
- What we see
- Questions we have
- Our experiences
- Thanks and appreciation
- Confession and confrontation

We *choose* what we will say and how we will say it.
To *confront* others means that you try to help them understand how their choices have affected you or someone else.

4. Effective communication

Respectful communication is good and pleases the Lord.
Disrespectful communication is sinful and often causes conflict.

Do not let any unwholesome talk come out of your mouths, but only what is helpful for **building others up** according to their needs, that it may benefit those who listen.

Ephesians 4:29

Lesson Goal:

To help students improve their communication skills so that they can prevent conflict.

Lesson Objectives:

By God's grace students will learn:

1. How to use the communication pie to help prevent conflict.
2. To consider the best time and place to communicate.

Key Principle:

Respectful communication is more likely to be heard.

Lesson Needs:

Bible
Student Activity Book #11
Worksheet Five—Using Respectful Words (Appendix C)

Begin with Prayer

Begin the lesson with prayer that your students will understand and apply principles of respectful and godly communication.

Review and Setting the Stage

- **Can anyone tell me what it means to communicate?** (To send and receive messages.)

- **What are some ways people communicate?** (Verbally and nonverbally; respectfully and disrespectfully.)

- **What is the difference between verbal and nonverbal communication?** (Verbal/with words; nonverbal/with actions.) **Can you give some examples?**

- **Can anyone remember what we communicate?** (Thoughts, ideas, beliefs, feelings, needs, desires, experiences, and appreciation, etc.)

- **Can you remember why we communicate?** (So other people can understand us; and to build others up, not to tear them down.)

You remembered some key points about communication. Good for you! Today we are going to talk more about how to communicate respectfully in order to prevent conflict. What you say and how you say it can often help to prevent conflict. However, there are some people with whom you will have conflict no matter how well you communicate. Always remember that you are not responsible for what others do or how they communicate; you are only responsible for how you choose to communicate to others. In this chapter you will see that **respectful communication is more likely to be heard**. More importantly, respectful communication glorifies the Lord. Therefore, it is important to take seriously your responsibility to communicate respectfully.

HEY DAD! GOTTA A GREAT IDEA!

Canoe Blues Continues

featuring

CARLOS & DAD

Before we explore respectful communication further, let's look in on Carlos and his father again. They still have some important things to learn about communication.

Teaching Tip

The story this week is a continuation of the story from Lesson 10.

Even though Carlos had apologized for being disrespectful to his father about their cancelled canoe trip, he was still feeling disappointed that their outing had been bumped again because his dad had to work overtime. As he sat on the back steps feeling sorry for himself, he heard his father calling to him.

"I'm out here, Dad. What do you want?"

"What's the matter with you?" his dad asked. "You look like you lost your best friend."

"Oh, nothin'," Carlos pouted. He was feeling as if he *had* lost his best friend—his dad! Carlos wondered if he would ever be as important to his dad as work seemed to be. Suddenly an idea came to him and he cheered up. Maybe his dad could take next Saturday off and they could still go canoeing. "I hope, I

hope, I hope," he thought.

"Hey, Dad! I have an idea! Since we can't go on our canoe trip today, how about if we go next Saturday? Please, Dad?"

"No, Carlos, I have to work late every night this week and next Saturday, too." His dad sounded impatient. "This is an important project I'm working on and I have to finish it before the end of the month."

Carlos lost his temper again. "Why can't we ever do fun things together? Why is it always work, work, work with you?" he yelled.

"Carlos, get off my case! You're always harping at me about my job! I'm tired of it. I'm going to work!" Dad yelled back. With that, he got in his car and pulled out of the driveway.

■ **How did Carlos choose to communicate?** (Disrespectfully)

Unfortunately, many people are like Carlos; they either blow up or clam up! Both ways of communicating are disrespectful and ineffective. Most people will not listen to or even try to understand a person who is pouting or throwing a temper tantrum.

Everyone needs to learn how to communicate in a respectful way so that God will be pleased and other people will listen. **Respectful communication is more likely to be heard.**

157

The Communication Pie

THE RIGHT **BODY** LANGUAGE

GOOD **LISTENING** SKILLS

THE RIGHT **WORDS** AND **TONE OF** VOICE.

RESPECTFUL **WORDS**

RESPECTFUL **TONE OF** VOICE

RESPECTFUL **LISTENING** SKILLS

RESPECTFUL **BODY** LANGUAGE

Before you send verbal or nonverbal messages to people, be sure to use the communication pie to help you communicate in a respectful way.

Communication Pie

Today we are going to learn how to use a tool that can help improve your communication skills and prevent conflict. This tool is called the *communication pie*. If you choose to use this tool, you may be surprised at how often people listen and respond to you respectfully.

The Communication Pie Consists of Four Pieces

- Respectful Words
- Respectful Tone of Voice
- Respectful Body Language
- Respectful Listening Skills

Two pieces of the communication pie involve verbal communication: words and tone of voice. The other two sections of the communication pie involve nonverbal communication: body language and listening skills.

Let's look carefully at each piece of this pie.

Using Respectful Words

Using respectful words is very important when you want someone to listen to you. Many people have developed the habit of using words to:

- grumble
- criticize
- gossip
- nag
- pout
- throw temper tantrums
- complain
- curse
- talk back
- whine
- argue

Do you find yourself struggling with some of these habits? If you do, I am sure that you often feel frustrated because people don't seem to listen to you. Even if they do listen, they may respond in an angry way to what you have said. You probably feel like giving up sometimes. Well, don't give up; I have good news!

Using disrespectful words is a choice, and remember, choices can change! You can choose to use different words—respectful words—to communicate. Respectful words "build others up according to their needs" (Eph. 4:29). They are truthful, clear, and encouraging. Even when they are used to confront, respectful words will promote healing and help people to grow.

Teaching Tip

It is important to clearly demonstrate examples of respectful and disrespectful communication using both words and tone of voice.

Using a Respectful Voice

If you want to be heard and understood, then you also need to be aware of how your tone of voice might sound to people. When you use a respectful and pleasant tone of voice as you would in a normal conversation, most people will listen to what you have to say. However, if you communicate with a wrong, sinful tone of voice that is argumentative, harsh, or disrespectful, you will probably find most people unwilling to hear you out. In addition, you may find yourself in trouble for communicating disrespectfully.

159

If you use respectful words but a disrespectful tone of voice, your communication will not be respectful or effective. The following are some examples of using the wrong tone of voice. (Teachers, dramatize the following examples to make the point.)

"Tha-a-a-nk you," sneered Mark.

"Well, I'm sor - r - r - ry," pouted Sandy.

"Can't you understand?" snarled Eric. (Implying that you are dumb!)

See how your tone of voice can affect your communication? Let's try those again. This time I'll use respectful words *and* a respectful tone of voice.

"Thank you," smiled Mark.

"I'm sorry for hurting your feelings," said Sandy gently.

"Is this hard to understand?" asked Eric.

Proverbs 15:1 says, "A gentle answer turns away wrath, but a harsh word stirs up anger." The Lord is telling us that we can stir up or calm down a quarrel with our tone of voice.

There are many ways that your tone of voice can stir up conflicts. You would be wise to avoid sending messages by whining, yelling, snarling, mumbling, pouting, snapping, or talking back by challenging, arguing, being rude, or speaking sharply.

■ **What was wrong with Carlos' tone of voice in the story when he spoke to his father?** (He was rude; he pouted and lost his temper.)

Avoid Using Double Messages

When you communicate to others, you need to make sure that your words and your voice are respectfully sending the same message. Let me explain. Sometimes your communication sends a double message, which means that you are sending one message with your words and another message with your tone of voice. Double messages are confusing. When Carlos was asked if something was bothering him, he pouted and said, "No!" Carlos sent a double message, because something *was* bothering him and his tone of voice said so. This is an easy and bad habit to get into. Instead of being understood as he wanted to be, Carlos' way of communicating created confusion and tension between him and his father. Sound familiar?

Your double messages will also cause confusion and tension, and you may find people unwilling to pay proper attention to you. On the other hand, when you use respectful words with a respectful tone of voice, you may be pleasantly surprised at how often people will listen to you and try to understand your point of view. You can begin to get a reputation for blessing others with your respectful words, which is an honor to the Lord and to you.

Using Respectful Body Language

Remember, **respectful communication is more likely to be heard,** and that applies to nonverbal communication as well as verbal communication. Like words and tone of voice, nonverbal messages (also called "body language") can be either respectful or disrespectful. With respectful body language, you will encourage people to pay attention to what you think and how you feel. Let's consider some right and wrong ways to use body language to communicate.

Eye Contact: We communicate a great deal with our eyes. Therefore, it is important to use eye contact respectfully. In many cultures looking at the person to whom you are talking is appropriate. Doing so shows that you are paying attention and trying to understand what is being said. (In some cultures, direct eye contact may not be appropriate or respectful.)

Your eye contact can be either respectful, inviting communication, or disrespectful, cutting off communication. Here are some examples:

Respectful:

- Look at the person to whom you are talking
- Look interested
- Look to show you are listening

Disrespectful:

- Roll your eyes
- Look away or look at something else
- Glare at the person

Facial Expressions: Facial expressions often show what is in your heart. A smiling facial expression is one that comes from a cheerful heart, and most people like to look at it. You can choose to look friendly, understanding, pleased, excited and so on. Facial expressions can also tell others when you feel scared, disappointed, angry, frustrated and sad, just to name a few.

Respectful:

- Friendly
- Smiling, cheery
- Understanding, compassionate
- Excited, happy
- Sad, disappointed (These can also be communicated disrespectfully.)

Disrespectful:

- Bored, frowning, pouting, glaring

Body Posture: Your body posture can also communicate that you are listening respectfully to what is being said. It is usually best to sit up or stand straight, face the person who is talking, and lean forward just a little. Doing so will communicate that you are taking an interest in what the other person is saying. On the other hand, when you slump down, fold your arms, turn away, or walk away, you send the message that you don't care about what is being said. You will probably develop a bad reputation, and other people may have a tendency to ignore what you have to say. Remember that you can choose what kind of body posture you will use.

Respectful:

- Sit up or stand straight
- Face the person who is talking
- Lean forward a little

Disrespectful:

- Slump down
- Look all around instead of at the person who is talking
- Fold arms
- Turn away or stomp off
- Glare and get too close to the other person

Gesture	Eye Contact	Facial Expression

Gestures: Gestures are another type of body language, and are usually done with your hands or arms. For instance, when you wave at a friend at a football game, and you motion to him to come sit next to you, you are using gestures in a friendly way. You might also wave at a person who is backing out of a parking place and is about to hit your bike, but you would probably wave your arms like crazy to signal to the person to stop before your bike gets crunched! However, when you shake your fist at someone, you are sending a threatening gesture, which may result in a conflict. Throwing things and slamming doors are also disrespectful gestures that cause conflict between you and others. As you can see, gestures can help or hinder good communication, as well as strengthen or tear down relationships.

Respectful:

- Wave at someone
- Motion to someone to come

Disrespectful:

- Shake your fist
- Throw things
- Slam doors

Let's practice sending messages using nonverbal communication. Each of you needs to communicate something to the class using body language. You can use eye contact, facial expressions, body posture, or gestures. Here are some ideas:

- I like you.
- I have a flat tire on my bike.
- I am so tired.
- I am so excited.

■ **What was it like communicating nonverbally? Did anyone understand your messages?**

■ **What could have made your communication more effective?**

When your words, tone of voice, and body language are working together in a respectful way, you will be a more effective communicator. Your **respectful communication is more likely to be heard.** You will also be taking the responsibility for trying to prevent fights and quarrels. You will probably find that you are not involved in as many conflicts as you used to be. And that's good!

We have one last piece of the pie to discuss.

Using Respectful Listening

Proverbs 18:13 says, "He who answers before listening—that is his folly and his shame." God wants his children to grow in righteousness and holiness instead of giving in to angry or careless speech. He desires that his children control their tongues and recognize when it is wise to keep quiet and listen.

First, listen to God. James 1:19-20 says, "Everyone should be quick to listen, slow to talk and slow to get angry, for man's anger does not bring about the righteous life that God desires." Be quick to listen to what God wants you to learn as you read his Word. God can help you grow in righteousness as you listen carefully to his Word and obey what it says.

Then listen carefully to others. Be quick to listen for the truth in what others say to you instead of getting angry when you don't like what you are hearing. One way to be a careful listener is to look at the person who is talking. This helps you to concentrate on what he or she is saying, and it sends a message that you are listening to what is being said. By listening, you are setting an example for the other person to listen to you when it's your turn to speak.

Another way to be a careful listener is to stop yourself from interrupting others when they are talking. Sometimes this is hard to do, especially if someone won't let you have a chance to talk. If this is the case, maybe you could use a respectful gesture to let the other person know that you have something you would like to say.

Sometimes you may not understand what someone is trying to communicate to you. When this happens, be a mirror and reflect back to the person what you have heard. It may also be necessary for you to tell them you don't understand their point. Just make sure you do it respectfully. For instance, you could say:

- "I am sorry, but I don't understand what you mean."
- "Could you explain to me what you mean by that?"

In addition, you will need to use self-control to listen when others say things that you don't like or don't want to hear. Your first reaction may be to blow up or clam up, but remember that communicating in these ways can cause conflict. Instead of blowing up or clamming up, pray that the Lord will help you listen for the truth and try to understand the other person's point of view, even if you don't agree with it. With God's help you can disagree without being disagreeable. Here are some ideas you could use to respond in a respectful way:

- "It's hard to hear you say that, but I see what you mean."
- "I can understand what you are saying, but I disagree."

Another important part of listening is responding to what was said, especially when a request is involved. Think about how you listen to your mother or father when they ask you to do something. The smartest and wisest response is to quickly and cheerfully obey. There may be

times, however, when you are doing something else that is important, and you may need to respectfully ask if you could respond to the request later. For example, you may be working on a homework assignment that must be completed by the next morning. This is a good reason to ask if you could finish your homework before you do what your parent has asked. If you listen and respond quickly and respectfully to other people's requests, you will encourage them to do the same for you.

These are just a few ideas that you can use to become a better listener. When you develop more effective listening skills, you will probably find that you will learn and understand more about people and they will be more likely to listen to you. A popular poster shows an old cowboy saying to a young boy, "If you're talkin' you ain't learnin'." That idea echoes King Solomon's proverb, where he says, "He who answers before listening—that is his folly and his shame" (Prov. 18:13).

Careful listening is an important part of respectful communication. Without it, people can easily be misunderstood and conflict is often the result. Let's say Prov. 18:13 together: "He who answers before listening—that is his folly and his shame."

Role Play Activity: You have been looking forward to the youth group picnic scheduled for this afternoon. Suddenly you realize that you are late, so you grab your jacket, tell your mother that you are leaving, and run to the church as fast as you can. When you get there, you realize that you forgot to bring your lunch for the picnic. Using the communication pie, call your mother and explain the situation. Make a respectful request that she bring your lunch to church.

The Best Time and Place

Most communication is relaxed and easy, but there are some things that may require that you plan when and where you will communicate. For example, if you want to ask permission to do something important or confront someone about a problem, it would not be wise to do it in front of others, or when the person is heading out of the door, or when the person is in the middle of doing something. At times like these, people may not be able to concentrate on what you are saying. Instead, choose a time when the person is not busy doing other things, or ask if there would be a good time to talk with him or her, so that you will have time to talk thoroughly about the situation. It is usually best to talk about serious things in private.

Once a good time and place have been selected, plan how to use the communication pie to help you to communicate respectfully. You may be pleased to discover that others may listen to you and take you more seriously. Remember that the way you communicate with others will often determine how they will communicate with you.

Let's say that a friend begins to yell at you, call you names, and glare at you. It happens repeatedly and you don't know why your friend is treating you this way. First, you could get help to plan how to confront your friend in a respectful way. Then choose the best time and place to talk with the person about his or her communication choices.

■ **What could you say to a friend who continually speaks disrespectfully to you?** ("I'd like to talk with you about something that is affecting our friendship. Is this a good time for us to talk?")

Always keep in mind that God wants your verbal and nonverbal communication to be helpful, to build others up, and to benefit your listeners. I encourage you to evaluate the way you communicate with others by using the communication pie. Ask the Lord to help you make necessary changes so that what you say and how you say it glorifies him and strengthens your relationships with others.

RESPECTFUL COMMUNICATION IS MORE LIKELY TO BE HEARD.

Wrapping It Up

We learned in this lesson that **respectful communication is more likely to be heard,** and the communication pie is a tool that can help you communicate respectfully. When you choose to use respectful words, tone of voice, and nonverbal body language to send messages, you will be taking responsibility to help prevent or resolve conflict between you and others. Remember, you can choose to communicate respectfully no matter what anyone else does! The Lord is clear in his Word that he values communication that builds up and benefits the listener. In addition, the Lord says that we are to be "quick to listen." Respectful listening demonstrates that you are trying to understand the other person's point of view, even if you don't agree with it.

Respectful communication is wise, it glorifies God, and it will help you stay on top of the slippery slope. What could be better?

Closing Prayer

Dear Lord, thank you that you have taught me in the Bible how I can communicate in a way that pleases you and builds others up. Sometimes when I get angry and frustrated, or when I simply want my own way, I say and do things that hurt others. Please forgive me for my selfishness and help me to communicate to everyone in a respectful way. Teach me to use respectful words with a respectful tone of voice. Help me to use the right kind of nonverbal communication that shows respect for others, and help me to become a better listener. Thank you for loving me enough to help me to change. In Jesus' name, Amen.

Making It Real

Assign one or more of the suggested activities for Lesson Eleven that are found in the Activities and Personal Application section of this lesson. Some of the activities are included in Student Activity Book #11.

Activities and Personal Application

Activities one and two can be found in Student Activity Book (SAB) #11.

1. What Are They Saying? (see SAB 11-9): Look at the body language of Carlos and his dad. Write their conversation in the balloons.

2. Taste the Pie (see SAB 11-10): Read each story and indicate whether the people used the ingredients for a good pie or a rotten pie.

3. Draw a picture showing yourself using the communication pie to communicate respectfully with another person. Write a brief explanation of what is happening in your picture.

4. In the week ahead use the communication pie to send and receive messages with people in your family. Write a paragraph that tells about what happened each time you communicated respectfully. Write down what you said, how you said it, how you listened, and how members of your family responded.

5. Play Simon Says in class. During the game the students should obey "Simon" only if he uses respectful communication when giving directions. Directions communicated disrespectfully are not to be obeyed.

6. Design a poster or a banner with the communication pie on it.

7. Divide the class into small groups. Have each group develop a five-minute role play that shows the characters using the communication pie to communicate respectfully or disrespectfully. Give the students an opportunity to act out their role plays. Then have the class evaluate the communication skills they observed.

Dig into the Word

Memory Verse:

Ephesians 4:29

Other Relevant Bible Verses:

Proverbs 15:1 and 4
Proverbs 12:18
Proverbs 16:23-24
Proverbs 18:13
Proverbs 21:23
Ephesians 4:15
James 1:19-20

Applicable Bible Stories:

Assign one or more of the following passages to help students analyze conflict situations in the Bible.

Abigail confronts David
(1 Samuel 25:1-35)

Daniel requests a more healthy diet
(Daniel 1:1-16)

Paul speaks to King Agrippa
(Acts 26:1-3)

The Lesson Summary

Bible Memory Verse

"Do not let any unwholesome talk come out of your mouths, but only what is helpful for building others up according to their needs, that it may benefit those who listen" (Eph. 4:29).

Key Principle

Respectful communication is more likely to be heard.

The Main Points of This Lesson

1. The communication pie

The communication pie consists of the following pieces:
- Respectful *Words*
- Respectful *Tone of Voice*
- Respectful *Body Language*
- Respectful *Listening*

Use *I messages* to communicate *words* in a respectful way.
If you use *respectful words* but a *disrespectful tone of voice*, you will be sending a *double message*. The *right tone of voice* is respectful and considerate.

Respectful body language:
- *Eye contact* means that you look respectfully at someone's eyes when you are speaking or listening to them.
- *Facial expressions* can tell others how you feel without using words.
- Your *body posture* will often show if you are taking an interest in what others are saying to you.
- *Gestures* are a type of body language that is usually done with hands and arms.

If you *listen respectfully* to others, they may be more willing to *listen* to you.

2. Consider the best time and place to communicate.

Choose a time when the other person is not busy or distracted.
It is usually best to ask permission, share feelings or concerns, make requests, or lovingly confront others *in private.*

Making a Respectful Appeal

> **God** opposes the proud but **gives grace** to the **humble.**
>
> 1Peter 5:5

Lesson Goal:

To help students understand that a respectful appeal is more effective than demanding their own way.

Lesson Objectives:

By God's grace students will learn:
1. What it means to make an appeal to someone.
2. How to make a respectful appeal.
3. When it is appropriate to make an appeal.
4. How to be a "STAR" at making appeals.

Key Principle:

A respectful appeal can prevent conflict.

Lesson Needs:

Bible
Student Activity Book #12
Worksheet Six—Making a Respectful
 Appeal—Appendix C

Begin with Prayer

Begin the lesson with prayer that God will help your students to resist the temptation to become argumentative and disrespectful. Ask him to give your students the wisdom and willingness to use the appeal process in a proper way.

Review and Setting the Stage

■ **Who remembers what the four pieces in the communication pie are called?** (Respectful words, respectful tone of voice, respectful body language, and respectful listening skills.)

Great! You remembered very well!

■ **Who used the communication pie to send messages to others this week? How did others respond to your respectful communication?** (Allow a few students to briefly share how they communicated respectfully and what happened as a result.)

■ **Have you ever felt afraid to talk to adults about decisions they make that affect you?**

■ **Do you ever feel like people don't care about what you think when they are making decisions?**

■ **Are there times when you wish you could explain your thoughts about what people are doing, but no one will listen?**

If you answered yes to any of those questions, I think you will appreciate today's lesson. We are going to talk about a way that you can *appeal* to someone to listen to you.

■ **Have you ever heard the word "appeal" used before? What do you think it means to make an appeal?**

Doubt About the Route

featuring
TAMEKA & CONNIE

THANKS FOR FILLING IN FOR ME. I DON'T KNOW WHAT I'D DO WITHOUT YOU.

Learning how to make **a respectful appeal can prevent conflict.** Listen to a story about a girl who could choose to make an appeal and prevent a conflict with her friend.

Tameka's friend Connie was going to camp for a week, and she asked Tameka to take responsibility for her paper route while she was gone. Tameka jumped at the chance to help her friend out as well as to make some money. The girls agreed that Tameka would deliver papers with Connie for a week so that she could learn the route.

"I can't wait to tell my parents that I've got a job! They'll be so proud of me!" said Tameka happily. "I'd better get home, Connie. Bye!"

When Tameka told her parents about her promise to deliver papers for Connie, she didn't get the reaction she thought she would.

"Tameka, you can't deliver papers for Connie next week," her mother said. "Dad has made arrangements to take his vacation next week. Our family is going to the beach, and we already have our reservations."

"Oh, no! I forgot all about our vacation!" Tameka moaned. "But I promised Connie, Mom!"

"You should have talked with us before you made such a promise. Connie will have to find someone else to help her."

Tameka sighed. "What am I going to tell Connie?"

Tameka has to make a choice as to how she is going to handle this problem. She could get angry and blame her parents, or she could lie to Connie about why she can't do the paper route. Worse yet, she could decide to break her promise to deliver the papers, but lead Connie to believe that the route is covered.

If Tameka chooses to do what is right, she will appeal to her friend to be released from her promise. Today we are going to talk about when and how to make a respectful appeal.

How to Ask for Something Using a STAR Appeal

You probably feel frustrated when decisions are made for you. You may be tempted to slip into the escape or attack zones, but that will only make matters worse. The wise thing to do is to use a respectful appeal to explain your point of view.

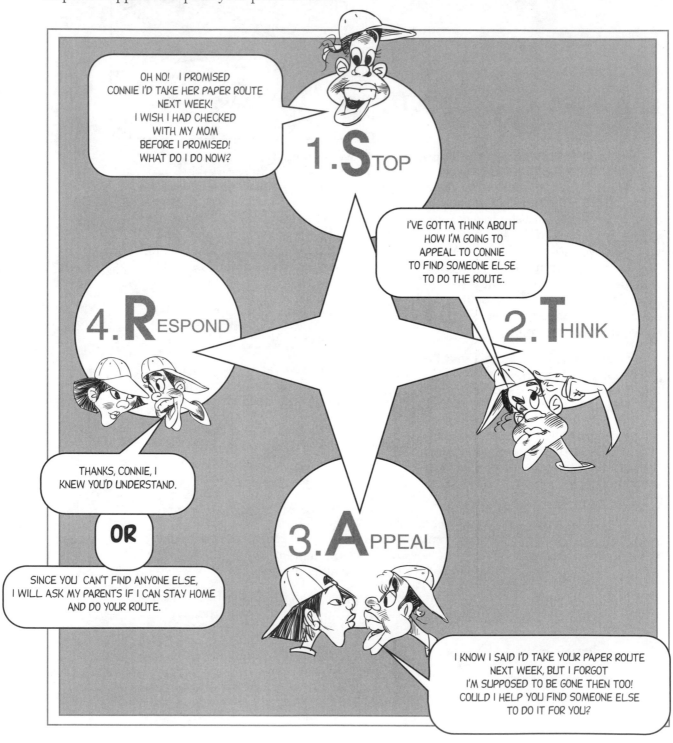

An Appeal

For our purposes, the word appeal will be defined in this way: *An appeal is a respectful request you make to others if you want them to consider your thoughts, feelings, or needs when they are making a decision.*

■ **Who do you think can make appeals?** (Anybody can make an appeal.)

That's right! Anybody can make an appeal. You can appeal to anyone who is making a decision that concerns you, including:

- Persons in authority (such as parents, teachers, policemen, government officials, church leaders, etc.)
- Peers (brothers, sisters, friends, etc.)
- Neighbors (anyone not already mentioned).

■ **To whom does Tameka need to make an appeal?** (To Connie)

Let's look at the two parts of a respectful appeal.

Making an Appeal

The first part of the appeal is the "I message." This part explains your reason for the appeal. In Tameka's case, she could say something like this:

"Connie, *I* am supposed to go to the beach with my family during the same week that you go to camp. When *I* promised to take your paper route, *I* didn't remember we would be gone that week."

Note that both sentences in the explanation use an "I message."

The second part of the appeal is the question. This part is the respectful request. It's the part that asks the person to consider your reason for making the appeal. In Tameka's situation, she could ask a number of questions. For instance:

"Connie, do you think you could find someone else to take your route for you that week?"

or

"Connie, would you mind if I tried to find someone else to do it for you?" (This would be especially appropriate if Connie had just moved into Tameka's neighborhood and didn't know anyone else to ask besides Tameka.)

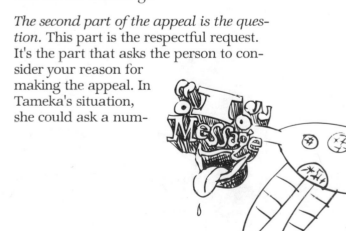

173

When to Appeal

There are good reasons, as well as selfish reasons, to make an appeal. If you want to communicate facts, concerns, needs, or even desires in a respectful way, then making an appeal is a proper thing to do. If you are making an appeal just to get your own way, then you are misusing the appeal process. For instance, you might try to appeal to your father to release you from cleaning up the yard because you are feeling lazy and you would rather watch television. Selfishness is at the root of that kind of appeal, and it is not a proper use of an appeal.

Let's look at a few situations when it is appropriate to make an appeal. (Note that each appeal begins with an *I message* and ends with a *question.*)

You Have Made an Unwise Commitment

There may be times when you make promises that will be difficult or impossible to fulfill. This can happen when you don't think before you make commitments. At times like this you will need to make a respectful appeal to be released from your unwise promise. Sometimes you may be released, while at other times you may need to make arrangements to follow through with your promise even if it is difficult to do so.

Example: Your school needs new playground equipment. In order to help raise money for this project, your class has challenged the teachers in your school to a basketball game. You promised your teacher that you would design and make all the posters that would be used to advertise the "big game." But you are not good at art, and you don't know how to design the posters. You hoped to convince your big brother to do it for you, because he is so good at this kind of thing. But he can't help you because he doesn't have time. You need to appeal to your teacher to be released from this project.

Making an appeal is a biblical way to be released from a commitment rather than breaking a promise (see Prov. 6:1-3).

I Message: "Miss Thomas, I know that I promised to design and make all the posters for the basketball game between the teachers and our class, but I am not good at art. I was hoping my brother could do them because they would be so cool, but he doesn't have time right now. I'm sorry I promised to do them when I knew I didn't know how."

Question: "Could you find someone else who is good at art to design and make the posters?"

It is likely that Miss Thomas will release you from your unwise commitment to do something that you knew you were not able to do. She will probably be thankful that you appealed to her instead of breaking your word.

Key: If you have made an unwise commitment, **a respectful appeal can prevent a conflict** that is likely to result if you break your promise.

You Have New Information

There are times when you need to communicate information or facts to someone about a decision that has already been made or that will be made. If you use an appeal, most people will be more willing to listen to you and consider the information that you are telling them. It is possible that some decisions could change.

Example: Your mother tells you to come home right after school tomorrow to babysit your little brother. But you just learned that you have been chosen for a part in the school play and you have to stay after school for an hour to rehearse. It is important to explain the facts to your mother.

I Message: "Mom, I have been chosen to play a part in the school play, so I need to stay after school tomorrow for an hour to rehearse."

Question: "Do you think you could ask Mrs. Jones to watch Bobby until I get home?"

When parents hear a respectful appeal they will usually respond respectfully. Keep in mind that this doesn't mean that you will always get what you want, but it does mean that parents and other adults may be more willing to listen to you.

Key: A respectful appeal can prevent a conflict by giving others all the information they need to make wise decisions.

You Have Been Wrongly Accused

You want people to do all they can to discover the truth before they give you the consequences for something you really did not do.

Example: Suppose you had borrowed one of your teacher's math books so you could practice a math concept that was difficult for you. You brought the book back the next morning and put it on the teacher's desk along with a thank you note. Later in the day the teacher asks you for the book so she can use it with another student. You tell her that you put it on her desk that morning. She doesn't believe you and tells you that you need to bring the math book back or replace it if you have lost it or ruined it. You need to respectfully explain that you didn't lose it.

I Message: "Mrs. Smith, I can understand why you think that I must still have the math book, but honestly, I put it on your desk this morning."

Question: "Would you mind looking for it a little longer before you make a final decision to have me replace the book?"

If you are ever in a situation like this one, you could consider replacing the book even though you had put it back on your teacher's desk (see Matt. 5:38–42).

■ **Why do think you that replacing the book might be the right thing to do?** (You were responsible for the book when you checked it out. That also means that you were responsible for returning it. Even though you did put it on your teacher's desk, it turned up missing while you were

responsible for it. Although it may not be necessary, replacing the book could be seen as a respectful and responsible choice. One way to have prevented this kind of problem is to have handed the book directly to the teacher when you returned it, instead of putting it on her desk.)

Key: Instead of escaping or attacking when you are wrongly accused, you can make **a respectful appeal that can prevent a conflict.**

Note: If you have a reputation for using the 5A's when you make wrong or sinful choices, then people will be more likely to believe you when you say that you have been wrongly accused. However, if you are in the habit of choosing to play the blame game, then people will probably question your honesty and think that you are just trying to avoid consequences.

You Have a Personal Preference

Everyone has personal preferences. In other words, we all have likes and dislikes. When you communicate those things in a respectful way, people are going to be more likely to listen to you. Sometimes they will make decisions based on your likes and dislikes. Other times they will make decisions based on what is good for you. Your responsibility is to communicate your preferences respectfully and resist the temptation to pout or argue if you don't get your own way.

Example: Your parents are planning a roller skating party for you and your friends to celebrate your birthday. When you find out about it, you are a little disappointed because you would rather have a swimming party. You need to respectfully explain to your parents what your preference would be and appeal to them to consider your thoughts about the matter.

I Message: "Mom and Dad, thanks for taking the time to plan a birthday party for me. A skating party sounds like fun, but I think a swimming party would be even more fun."

Question: "Could we go to the pool instead?"

It is possible that your parents would be willing to plan a swimming party instead of a skating party. However, they may know that the pool is closed for repairs so a swimming party would not be possible. In either case, you could thank your parents for wanting to make your birthday a fun time.

Key: Making a respectful appeal can prevent conflict by helping others to understand your likes and dislikes.

176

You Are Concerned for Someone Else

Have you ever been in a situation when you felt worried or concerned about choices other people were making? For instance, you might fear that your parents' marriage problems may lead to divorce. Or maybe you are concerned about a friend who is planning to shoplift. Or perhaps you overheard a friend talking about doing something that would hurt another friend. Or your sister tells you that she thinks about hurting herself. These are very serious situations. In each one, and in others like them, you can appeal to the person to make the right choice—a choice that would not be hurtful or sinful. You need to understand that you are not responsible for the choice the person makes, only for making your appeal in a respectful way.

Example: You hear your brother talking to one of his friends about their plan to sneak out of the house on Friday night to go to another friend's house for a party. You have heard about this party, too, and you are concerned that your brother will get in trouble or get hurt if he chooses to go. You can appeal to your brother to make the right choice and stay away from the party.

I Message: "Mike, I heard you and Ted talking about going to Ron's party this Friday night. You know that Mom and Dad said we are not allowed to go to his parties, and you could get hurt if you go. Ron's parties have a bad reputation. I just don't want to see you get in trouble! Besides, if you go, you'll disobey God since Mom and Dad told you not to go. And that's serious!"

Question: "Won't you please reconsider and stay home Friday night?"

Making an appeal in a situation like this can be a hard thing to do. A consequence for making such an appeal may be a "blow up," but there's a good reason for the conflict. You are not trying to get your own way, but rather you are showing a loving concern for someone you care about. No matter what choice the person makes, your choice to appeal in a respectful way is good. Remember that success is not a matter of convincing a person to change his or her mind. You will be successful if your appeal is respectful.

Key: A respectful appeal can prevent conflict by helping others to turn away from wrong choices.

These examples are only five situations when it is appropriate to use an appeal. There will be many times in your life when making an appeal will help others to listen to you and consider your request.

The STAR Appeal

I am going to teach you an easy way to remember the parts of a respectful appeal. It's called the STAR Appeal. It goes like this:

- Stop
- Think
- Appeal
- Respond respectfully

Stop

Stop yourself from choosing to respond in a way that will cause conflict. (For example, lose your temper, whine, nag, argue, challenge, make excuses, etc.)

Think

Think about why you want to appeal and what words to use. Ask yourself the following questions:

- Have I made an unwise promise?
- Do I have facts or information that others need to know about?
- Have I been accused of something I didn't do?
- Do I have a personal preference that I want someone to consider?

- Am I concerned about a choice someone else is going to make?
- What words should I use to appeal?

I Message:_____

_____

_____

Question: _____

_____

_____

Appeal

Make your appeal in a respectful way, using *I messages* and *questions* to communicate facts, concerns, and preferences.

Respond Respectfully

Respond respectfully! Accept the decision whether the appeal is granted or not. This is an important part of the appeal. Your appeal may be granted or it may not be granted. Before you make your appeal, ask yourself these questions:

What will I say if my appeal is granted?

- "Thank you for considering my appeal."

- "I appreciate your willingness to change your mind."
- "Thank you for listening to my concerns and taking them into consideration."

What will I say if my appeal is not granted?

- "I don't agree with your decision, but I am willing to accept it."

The STAR Appeal is fairly simple, and it is often the easiest way to prevent unnecessary conflict. When you use it for proper reasons and at the right time, you will pleased to find out that most people are willing to listen to a respectful appeal.

Wrapping It Up

You have learned what an appeal is, when to use it, and how to communicate it respectfully. Instead of demanding your own way and throwing a temper tantrum if you don't get it, you can choose to make a wise and respectful appeal. You will find there are many benefits to making a STAR Appeal, such as:

- **A respectful appeal can prevent conflict.**

- A respectful appeal can build trust between you and the person to whom you are making the appeal.
- Most people will usually listen to a respectful appeal.
- A respectful appeal is more likely to be granted than a disrespectful demand.
- A respectful appeal glorifies the Lord.

Closing Prayer

Dear Lord, I am glad that I have learned about a way to appeal to people so that they will listen to me more often. Sometimes I feel frustrated when people don't consider my thoughts, feelings, needs, or desires. I confess that sometimes I don't communicate them in a respectful way. Please forgive me for being demanding and disrespectful. Help me to use the STAR Appeal to make an appeal when I need to. Please help me to communicate so others will listen to me. Thank you for giving me the strength to do what is right. In Jesus' name,
Amen.

Making It Real

Assign one or more of the suggested activities for Lesson Twelve that are found in the Activities and Personal Application section of this lesson. Most of the activities are included in Student Activity Book #12.

Activities and Personal Application

Activities one and two can be found in Student Activity Book (SAB) #12.

1. What Will You Do When? (see SAB 12-9): Read each situation and decide what you will do to solve the problem. Then match the reasons for an appeal with the story situations. (Answers: 1-A 2-E 3-B 4-C 5-D)

2. Real Appeal (see SAB 12-10): In each situation, read the appeal and then rewrite it in your own words.

3. Think about a situation where making an appeal would be an appropriate thing to do.

- Think about why an appeal is necessary. Think about who the best person would be to hear your appeal.

- Think about what words you could use to appeal respectfully. If you need advice, who would be the best person to help you?

- Complete the worksheet titled "Making a Respectful Appeal" (Appendix C).

- Plan when and how you will make the appeal. Will you make your appeal in person or will you write a letter? When would be the best time to appeal?

- Follow through on your plan to make your appeal. Be prepared to respond respectfully whether or not your appeal is granted.

- Evaluate your appeal. Was it respectful? Did the person to whom you made your appeal listen to you?

- Do you believe that your appeal pleased and glorified God?

Dig into the Word

Memory Verse:

1 Peter 5:5

Other Relevant Bible Verses:

Proverbs 6:1-3

Applicable Bible Stories:

Assign one or more of the following passages to help students analyze conflict situations in the Bible.

Abraham appealing to God for Sodom and Gomorrah
(Gen. 18:16-33)

Ruth appealing to Naomi
(Ruth 1:11-18)

Daniel appealing to official
(Dan. 1:8-16)

Paul appealing to Festus
(Acts 25:10-11)

The Lesson Summary

Bible Memory Verse

"God opposes the proud but gives grace to the humble" (1 Pet. 5:5).

Key Principle

A respectful appeal can prevent conflict.

The Main Points of This Lesson

1. What it means to make an appeal

An appeal is a respectful request that you make to a person when you want him or her to consider your thoughts or feelings when making a decision.
Anyone can make an appeal to *people in authority, peers, or anyone else.*

2. How to make an appeal

The two parts of an appeal are the *I message* and *the question.*

3. When to make an appeal

The five reasons for an appeal are:
- I have made an *unwise promise.*
- I have *facts or information* that others need to know about.
- I have been *accused* of something I didn't do.
- I have a *personal preference* that I want someone to consider.
- I am *concerned* about a choice someone else is going to make.

4. How to make a STAR Appeal

STAR stands for:
- *Stop* yourself from choosing to say or do something that will cause a conflict.
- *Think* about why you want to appeal and what words you will use.
- *Appeal* in a respectful way using "I messages" and questions to communicate facts, concerns, and preferences.
- *Respond respectfully* and accept the decision without arguing, whether your appeal is granted or not.

Often a wise and respectful appeal can *glorify God, help prevent conflict, and build trust* between you and the person to whom you are making the appeal.

> A RESPECTFUL APPEAL CAN PREVENT CONFLICT.

When and How to Go and Get Help

> Pride only breeds quarrels, but **wisdom** is found in those who **take advice**.
>
> Proverbs 13:10

As we learned in studying the slippery slope, there are three basic ways that you can respond to conflict. You can escape, you can attack, or you can work out your differences in a way that will glorify God. We learned many things that can help you resolve conflicts in a way that pleases the Lord. We have discussed:

- How you can stay on top of the slippery slope rather than slip into the escape or attack zones.
- What conflict is and where it comes from.
- The fact that your choices may cause or prevent most of your conflicts, and that you will receive either good or bad consequences depending on the choices you make.
- How your conflicts give you an opportunity to glorify God by the way you treat other people.
- The importance of making wise-way choices instead of my-way choices that satisfy your sinful desires.
- How playing the blame game makes conflicts worse, but using the 5A's can lead to forgiveness and reconciliation.
- How to seek and give the four promises of forgiveness so that relationships can be restored.
- How to alter your choices so that you don't make the same sinful choices again and again.
- The fact that you can prevent or resolve many conflicts by communicating respectfully.
- How you can use an appeal to ask people to release you from an unwise commitment or reconsider a decision they are about to make.

As we have discussed these things, most of our attention has been devoted to ways that you can talk things out in private with another person. But as we all know, there will probably be times when we won't be able to overlook a conflict or reach an agreement by talking in private. This is when you will need to use the third step in the work-it-out zone, which is to *go and get help* from another person. Remember that there are three ways to get help.

Coaching

One way to get help is to ask someone else to give you advice or coach you on how you can do a better job of talking privately with the person who disagrees with you. There may be several people who could give you this advice, including your parents, your pastor, a teacher, or a wise friend. These people can help you plan your words and choose the best time and place to talk to the other person. They can also help you plan what you can do if the other person does not want to be reconciled.

How should you ask someone for help? Should you go tell on the other person, or blame someone else for the problem? As we have already learned, these choices will not help the situation! Instead, you should go to the person you are asking for help and say something like this:

"Mom, Terry and I are having a problem. Can you help me work it out?"

You should then explain your problem, talking first about what you have done wrong ("getting the log out of your own eye," as God's Word says to do). When you start to describe what the other person has done wrong, be careful not to exaggerate or place all of the blame on him or her. Once the person coaching you has heard your description, he or she should be able to suggest some things that you may be able to do to resolve the conflict on your own.

Mediation

Let's say that you follow your advisor's suggestions and do all of the right things, but you still can't settle your conflict with the other person. Either you won't forgive each other, or you can't agree about what you are quarreling over. What can you do then? This is a good time for you to get the second kind of help, which Jesus describes in Matthew 18:16. We call this mediation. A mediator meets and talks with both you and the person with whom you are disagreeing. A mediator should be someone you and the other person trust, respect, and will listen to. Both of you can explain your view of the problem to this person, and he or she can suggest helpful ways for you to come to an agreement. It is important to listen carefully to the mediator's advice. As Proverbs 13:10 says: "Pride only breeds quarrels, but wisdom is found in those who take advice" (Prov. 13:10).

When you first ask the mediator for help, you should be careful not to give lots of details about what the other person did that upset you. Instead, just explain the problem in general and then wait until you and the other person are with the mediator before you go into detail. (This will give the other person a chance to hear what you say and respond to it.) As you give your explanation of what happened, remember to start by telling what you did wrong before you talk about what the other person did.

For example, let's say that Eric has been angry with his friend Terry. When they get together with a mediator, who might be a mutual friend, the mediator could say, "Eric, would you start by describing what you have done to hurt Terry?"

Eric might then say, "Terry, I admit I have said some mean things about you behind your back. I have been telling our friends that you can't be trusted, and I have tried to get them to ignore you because of this conflict. I'm sorry I have hurt your reputation. I will go back to each one of them and explain what I did wrong, and I will encourage them to stay friends with you. Will you please forgive me? Next time I won't talk behind your back. Instead I'll come talk to you if I am upset about something."

Hopefully, Terry would forgive Eric and also confess what he did wrong. But if he doesn't, the mediator can give Eric an opportunity to confront Terry in a respectful way. The mediator might say,

"Eric, is there something that Terry did that you believe was wrong, too?" Then Eric could answer:

"Yes. Terry, I felt frustrated when you wouldn't return my new CD that I let you borrow. It seemed like you had some excuse for not giving it back, and then I heard from Mark that you lost it. This makes it hard for me to trust what you say."

The mediator could then encourage Terry to take responsibility for his part in the conflict. He might say "Terry, why don't you use the 5A's to describe your role in this situation." Terry might then say something like this:

"Eric, I admit that I lost the new CD you loaned me, and then I made excuses for not giving it back to you like I said I would. I am sorry for lying to you. I understand why you don't feel like you can trust what I say. I can't give you the CD I lost, but I will give you the money to get a new one. I'll bring it to your house as soon as I can earn it. Will you forgive me? Next time I'll be more careful with things I borrow from you, and I won't lie to you again, either."

If both Eric and Terry are wise and take the mediator's advice to talk to each other like this, they will probably be able to forgive one another and work out their differences. This is why it is wise to find a mediator when you need help in resolving a conflict!

Arbitration

It's usually best for people to resolve a conflict by coming to a voluntary agreement, either on their own or with the help of a mediator. But sometimes this just won't happen. For example, let's say that Eric and Terry forgive one another, but they can't come to an agreement about who is responsible for replacing the CD. What can they do? This is when they need to get a third type of help, which is called arbitration. They would ask the person who has been mediating to go one step further and make the decision about who should replace the CD. Both boys would need to submit to that decision without arguing, and then they should move on with their friendship.

As you can see, there are always ways to resolve a conflict constructively if everyone is willing to obey God's Word and follow the conflict resolution processes he teaches us through the Bible. When we cannot overlook offenses or resolve conflicts on our own, we should get whatever help we need from others to lay the matter to rest. This can sometimes take time and effort, but it will always please God when we try to resolve conflicts the way he commands. When we do that, we can experience the joy and satisfaction that come from being a peacemaker. Therefore, let's pray that the Lord will help us do all the things that we have learned in these lessons so that Jesus' promise will come true in our lives:

"Blessed are the peacemakers, for they
shall be called the children of God" (Matt. 5:9, KJV).

Appendix A

Additional Role Play Scenarios

Use the following role play teasers to act out appropriate responses to conflict. At times you will be demonstrating how to handle a conflict; at other times you will show how to prevent a conflict.

- You pushed another student down at recess.

- You talked back to your mom.

- A friend borrowed your bike and got it all muddy.

- You acted bossy when you were playing a game with a friend.

- You borrowed your friend's favorite tape and lost it.

- You promised to turn in your brother's math homework because he is sick. You forgot to turn it in for him.

- You chose to come home late from a friend's house. Your parents are eating dinner when you walk in the house.

- You and and a friend avoided another girl out on the playground.

- You lied to your teacher, saying you turned in your workbook when you know that you did not.

- Your father told you to mow the lawn, but you didn't do it. You went to a football game with your friend instead.

- You lost your friend's baseball mitt.

- You promised to pick up a friend to go to a movie. You forgot all about it and went to the movie without her.

- You want to go roller skating with a friend, but your mother says no.

- You and your brother want to watch different TV shows at the same time.

- Your mother is talking on the phone and you want to ask her a question.

- Your friend asks you to go bike riding, but you know that you have homework to do.

- Your father was not aware of how he embarrassed you when he teased you in front of a group of friends.

- Your brother walked up to you and hit you for no apparent reason.

Working with Parents

Dear Teachers,

If you are teaching *The Young Peacemaker* program in a private school or a church Sunday School, you may use the letter found on the next page to send to your students' parents. This letter will provide parents with an overview of the program and explain ways they can reinforce peacemaking principles with their children. I recommend that this letter be sent home before you teach the first lesson, or that it be given to parents at an early informational meeting where you explain the program and answer any questions they may have.

As you teach *The Young Peacemaker* program, please encourage your students to take their Student Activity Books (or reproducible Student Activity Sheets) home so they can review them with their parents. This will help parents to be aware of the principles their children are learning and explore together what the Bible says about conflict resolution. This learning process will be especially effective if parents actually work through assigned activities with their children.

If you want to bring the parents into the learning process even more, you could provide each family with a copy of "*The Peacemaker*," which provides an adult version of the principles presented in the children's material. This inexpensive brochure may be purchased through Peacemaker Ministries.

You can also provide parents with a copy of the Twelve Key Principles that the children will learn through this program. Encourage the parents to post this list in a special place in their home so it can be referred to often. This handout is found at the end of Appendix B.

I hope you will enjoy teaching *The Young Peacemaker* to your students. I also hope that as your students and their families take these principles to heart, they will enjoy the rich blessings of being peacemakers in their homes, work places, schools, churches and neighborhoods. May the Lord bless your efforts.

Sincerely,

Corlette Sande

A Letter to Parents

Dear Parent,

Greetings! I would like to introduce myself. I am Corlette Sande, author of the conflict resolution program for children called *The Young Peacemaker*. During the next few weeks, your child's teacher is going to use *The Young Peacemaker* program to explore principles of conflict resolution that are taught in the Bible. Through this program, your child will learn that repentance, confession and forgiveness are the heartbeat of conflict resolution. Your child will also discover biblical answers to questions like:

- What is at the heart of conflict?
- Is it possible to honor God by my response to conflict?
- How can I take responsibility for my contribution to a conflict?
- How can I go and talk to someone if we are in a fight?
- How can we become friends again if there's a wall between us?

Students of all ages have learned life-changing answers to these questions from the principles taught in *The Young Peacemaker*. As a mother and former school teacher and counselor, I have found that most students from kindergarten through twelfth grade have trouble responding to conflict in a constructive manner. Their natural tendency is to run away from the problem or attack their opponent verbally or physically. Neither of these extremes will ever resolve conflict. When children respond to conflict by escaping or attacking, they become more angry, more bitter, and more convinced that their position is right, even if it isn't.

The opposite is true as well. When children learn to view conflict as an opportunity to bring glory to the Lord and decide to handle their problems responsibly, anger and bitterness dissipate and true conflict resolution can occur. Even if an opponent doesn't cooperate, the child who chooses to repent, confess, and forgive can be confident that he or she has been faithful to the Lord and obedient to his will. This is success in God's eyes.

If you would like additional understanding of God's answers to these questions, I encourage you to read *The Peacemaker: A Biblical Guide to Resolving Personal Conflict* (Baker Books, 2nd Ed. 1997), which was written by my husband, Ken. Through his book you can learn even more about biblical conflict resolution and discover ways that you can be a positive example to your children. As you and your children put God's peacemaking principles into practice, your home can increasingly become a place of peace.

Throughout the next twelve weeks your child's teacher will be sending home handouts for you to review. Some will be primarily for your information so you can be aware of what your child has learned about peacemaking each week. Other handouts will be activity sheets that you can help your child complete. These studies and activities are for the purpose of reinforcing the principles from each lesson. Of course, the best way to reinforce biblical peacemaking principles for your child is to demonstrate them in your own life.

I pray that you and your child will know the blessing that comes from being a peacemaker for the Lord's sake!

Sincerely,

Corlette Sande

Twelve Key Principles for Young Peacemakers

1. Conflict is a slippery slope.

2. Conflict starts in the heart.

3. Choices have consequences.

4. Wise-way choices are better than my-way choices.

5. The blame game makes conflict worse.

6. Conflict is an opportunity.

7. The 5A's can resolve conflict.

8. Forgiveness is a choice.

9. It's never too late to start doing what's right.

10. Think before you speak.

11. Respectful communication is more likely to be heard.

12. A respectful appeal can prevent conflict.

Reinforcement Worksheets

You can use these worksheets with children to help them work through a conflict in which they are involved. Once they understand how to use the worksheets, keep a supply of them at a peace table or problem-solving corner in your home or classroom so children can use them independently.

Identifying Good and Bad Choices

Think of several examples of good and bad choices and list them in the appropriate column.

GOOD CHOICES   **BAD CHOICES**

"The good man brings good out of the good stored up in his heart, and the evil man brings evil things out of the evil stored up in his heart. For out of the overflow of his heart his mouth speaks" (Luke 6:45).

Choices Have Consequences

Write down an example of a good choice and the opposite bad choice in the spaces provided. Then make a list of the predictable consequences for both choices.

GOOD CHOICE:

GOOD CONSEQUENCES:

BAD CHOICE:

BAD CONSEQUENCES:

"Do not deceive yourselves; no one makes a fool of God. A man will reap exactly what he plants" (Gal. 6:7, TEV).

Using the 5A's

Using the 5A's, write a confession to someone you have wronged.

Admit what I did wrong.
Apologize for how my choice affected you.
Accept the consequences.
Ask for forgiveness.
Alter (change) my choice in the future.

I admit I _____

_____

I am sorry for _____

_____

I know that what I did was wrong and I understand why I need to _____

_____

Will you please forgive me?

With God's help, next time I will _____

_____

"He who conceals his sins does not prosper, but whoever confesses and renounces them finds mercy" (Prov. 28:13).

"If we confess our sins, he is faithful and just and will forgive us our sins and purify us from all unrighteousness" (1 John 1:9).

Altering Choices—the STAY Plan

Use the STAY Plan to think about how you can alter one of your bad choices to a good choice.

Stop:

Identify the choice that caused the conflict: _____.

Identify the root desire of the choice: _____.

Think:

List some possible choices (good and bad) that you could make in the future, and predict their consequences. Pray that God will help you to think of wise-way choices that would please him.

	CHOICE	**CONSEQUENCES**
1.	_____	_____
2.	_____	_____
3.	_____	_____
4.	_____	_____
5.	_____	_____

Now circle the good choices. Ask God to help you choose the best choice and then put a star beside it.

Act:

Ask God to help you plan how to put your best choice into action. Write your plan below, then pray for strength to follow through with it.

_____

_____

_____

Yea!

Remember to thank the Lord if your plan works.

"Those who plan what is good find love and faithfulness" (Prov. 14:22).

Using Respectful Words

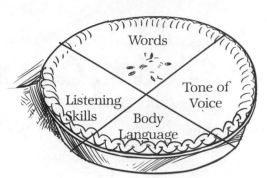

Prepare to go and talk to someone about a conflict by completing the following "I messages."

I feel _____ because _____

_____

I feel _____ because _____

_____

I felt _____ when _____

_____

I felt _____ when _____

_____

I felt _____ when _____

_____

I think _____

_____

I think _____

_____

I think _____

_____

I need _____

_____

I need _____

_____

I would like _____

_____

 "Do not let any unwholesome talk come out of your mouths, but only what is helpful for building others up according to their needs, that it may benefit those who listen" (Eph. 4:29).

Making a STAR Appeal

Stop

Stop yourself from choosing to say or do something that will cause conflict. (For example, lose your temper, whine, nag argue, challenge, make excuses, etc.)

Think

Think about why you want to appeal and what words to use. Ask yourself the following questions:

- Have I made an unwise promise?
- Do I have facts or information that others need to know about?
- Have I been accused of something I didn't do?
- Do I have a personal preference that I want someone to consider?
- Am I concerned about a choice someone else is going to make?
- What words should I use to appeal?

Appeal

Make your appeal in a respectful way, using I messages and questions to communicate facts, concerns and preferences.

I message: _____

_____

_____

Question: _____

_____

Respond Respectfully

Plan to respond respectfully! Accept the decision, whether the appeal is granted or not. Before you make your appeal, ask yourself these questions:

What will I say if my appeal is granted?_____

_____

What will I say if my appeal is not granted? _____

_____

"God opposes the proud, but gives grace to the humble" (1 Peter 5:5).